COOPERATING WITH GOD

How to Partner with Your Creator for Supernatural Results

BY RANDY CLARK

Cooperating With God
How To Partner With Your
Creator For Supernatural Results
© 2014 by Randy Clark

ISBN: 978-1-7324247-0-8

All rights reserved. No part of this book may be reproduced in any form or by any electronic or mechanical means, including information storage and retrieval systems, without written permission from the author, except in the case of a reviewer, who may quote brief passages embodied in critical articles or in a review.

Unless otherwise noted, all Scripture quotations are taken from the *Holy Bible*, New Living Translation, Copyright © 1996. Used by permission of Tyndale House Publishers, Inc., Wheaton, Illinois 60189. All rights reserved.

Scripture quotations marked (NKJV) are taken from the New King James Version® of the Bible. Copyright © 1982 by Thomas Nelson Inc.: Nashville. Used by permission. All rights reserved.

Scripture quotations marked (AMP) are taken from the Amplified Bible, Copyright © 1954, 1958, 1962, 1964, 1965, 1987 by The Lockman Foundation. Used by permission. (www.Lockman.org)

Underlining in Scripture quotations indicates the author's emphasis. For more resources by the author, go to his website:

www.RandyClark.info

Contents

1. The Sovereignty of God 1

2. Salvation 23

3. Guidance 33

4. Answered Prayer 55

5. Financial Provision 71

6. Soulwinning 93

7. Marriage 111

8. Healing 125

9. Preparing To Serve 149

10. Holy Spirit Power 165

1. The Sovereignty of God

Life is full of questions. "Why doesn't God seem to be answering my prayers?" Why can't I figure out what God wants me to do?" "Is there anything I can do to save my marriage?" "Will God really forgive me for what I have done?" "How can I have enough money to take care of my needs?" "How can I figure out a practical way to serve God?" "What can I do to be healed?" "How can I experience the power of the Holy Spirit?" "How can I overcome my fear of sharing my faith?"

Do any of those questions ring true in your life? Many of us struggle to understand how to balance the sovereignty of God with our actions. We wonder if our prayers are not answered simply because our request is not the will of God. We question whether a divorce may be part of God's plan for our lives. We sometimes assume the lack of good things happening is always an indication those things are outside the will of God. But maybe we need to make some right decisions and take some appropriate action to cooperate with God. Perhaps God has established some principles in His word for us to follow to see His will accomplished. I know He wants His will to be done. Jesus taught His disciples to pray for that to happen.

> **Pray like this: Our Father in heaven, may your name be kept holy. May your Kingdom come soon. May your will be done on earth, as it is in heaven. (Matthew 6:9-10)**

COOPERATION PRODUCES RESULTS

Moses faced a crisis. He had confronted Pharaoh repeatedly with God's demand to let the people of Israel go free from the slavery of Egypt. After the tenth and final plague, the death of the firstborn, Pharaoh relented and told them to go. He quickly changed his mind after they left, however, and his army was closing in on Moses and the approximately two million Israelites. The Red Sea loomed ahead of Moses. Pharaoh's army was behind. The situation looked grim. Moses was crying out to God, expecting <u>Him</u> to do something. But God had a different plan.

> **But Moses told the people, "Don't be afraid. Just stand still and watch the Lord rescue you today. The Egyptians you see today will never be seen again. The Lord himself will fight for you. Just stay calm." Then the Lord said to Moses, "Why are you crying out to me? Tell the people to get moving! Pick up your staff and raise your hand over the sea. Divide the water so the Israelites can walk through the middle of the sea on dry ground. (Exodus 14:13–16)**

God told Moses they could all cross the Red Sea on dry ground. When Moses looked ahead, he saw the vast expanse of water. Underneath the water was ground, but it certainly wasn't dry. Every minute that ticked by brought the Egyptian army closer. Some of the Israelites had already decided they were going to die in the wilderness. They were ready to lead a rebellion against Moses. Moses felt the incredible burden of responsibility for an entire nation.

What was the will of God? The will of God was for the nation of Israel to cross the Red Sea on dry ground. But there was no dry ground, only water. Was it God's fault that the Red Sea remained an obstacle? Or was it going to take cooperation from Moses for God's will to be accomplished? Nothing changed until Moses lifted up the staff in his hand and stretched it out over the sea.

> **Then Moses raised his hand over the sea, and the Lord opened up a path through the water with a strong east wind. The wind blew all that night, turning the seabed into dry land. So the people of Israel walked through the middle of the sea on dry ground, with walls of water on each side! (Exodus 14:21-22)**

<u>God's will could not be accomplished until Moses was willing to cooperate.</u> If Moses had refused to stretch his hand out over the sea, the sea would never have parted. God's power parted the sea and dried the ground, but Moses had a part to play. <u>He had to cooperate with God.</u>

SOVEREIGNTY DEMONSTRATED

Can God do anything He wants? Does His will always come to pass no matter what anybody does or does not do? If He wants something to happen, does He always make it happen? If He does not want something to happen, does He always stop it from coming to pass? If God's sovereignty is without restraint, we are absolved of all responsibility for our actions. If that is the case, we don't have to pray. We don't have to live right. We can do whatever we want. If God's will is always going to happen because of His sovereignty, we are nothing more than puppets for Him to manipulate.

This book may challenge your belief about the sovereignty of God. If you weren't sure how to respond to the questions in the last paragraph, this book will provide you with answers from Scripture that prove, at times, our cooperation is required for God's will to be manifested. You will see that we have a part to play in God's master plan for our lives. Our lack of cooperation can hinder or even prevent the will of God from being accomplished. To understand how this all works, we need to begin in the book of beginnings.

> **Then God said, "Let Us make man in Our image, according to Our likeness; let them have dominion over the fish of the sea, over the birds of the air, and over the cattle, over all the earth and over every creeping thing that creeps on the earth." So God created man in His own image; in the image of God He created him; male and female He created them. Then God blessed them, and God said to them, "Be fruitful and multiply; fill the earth and subdue it; have dominion over the fish of the sea, over the birds of the air, and over every living thing**

> that moves on the earth." (Genesis 1:26-28)
> (NKJV)

After creating Adam and Eve, God told them to exercise dominion over everything He had created. God expected His creation, Adam and Eve, to **work together with Him** to establish His will on the earth. They were to be in charge of the earth and everything God had created on the earth. God owned the earth because He created it. But He gave the responsibility and authority to run the earth to Adam and Eve and all those who would follow.

> May you be blessed by the Lord, who made heaven and earth. The heavens belong to the Lord, but he has given the earth to all humanity. (Psalm 115:15-16)

It is like God gave Adam and Eve a lease on the earth. I leased a house one time. Because I had a legal contract to lease the house for a period of time, the owner could not interfere with my lifestyle inside the house even though I did not own the house. My wife and I made all the decisions about what we did inside. The owner couldn't come inside at any time and tell us what to eat for dinner, how to arrange our furniture, or who we could talk to on the phone. The owner had given us the right to make those decisions as long as we had a valid lease.

God gave Adam and Eve and their descendants the right to make decisions while they live on the earth under that lease arrangement, even if those decisions are not in line with His will. God's creation could live in peace, health and prosperity if they cooperated with God. However, if they refused to cooperate with God, calamity could occur even though it was not the will of God.

> **Then the Lord God took the man and put him in the garden of Eden to tend and keep it. And the Lord God commanded the man, saying, "Of every tree of the garden you may freely eat; but of the tree of the knowledge of good and evil you shall not eat, for in the day that you**

eat of it you shall surely die." (Genesis 2:15–17) (NKJV)

God clearly made known His will. Do not eat of the tree of the knowledge of good and evil. The Hebrew word translated "evil" means "adversity, affliction, bad, calamity, grief, hurt, harm and trouble." God told Adam not to eat from that tree because He did not want His creation to obtain the ability to produce "adversity, affliction, bad, calamity, grief, hurt, harm and trouble." Adam lived in perfect harmony with His Father. He only knew about the blessings of God. God warned him not to partake of the fruit of the tree of the knowledge of good and evil. God loved Adam and did not want him to suffer from "adversity, affliction, bad, calamity, grief, hurt, harm and trouble." It was not the will of God for Adam or Eve to sin. God did not create mankind so they could suffer the consequences of sin.

Satan was once the highest ranking angel of God's angelic army when he was known as Lucifer. God had placed Lucifer in a position of great authority. He was God's most beautiful creation, full of wisdom, with perfect access to God. One day Lucifer made a decision to try to overthrow God. As a result, God stripped Lucifer of all authority and cast him to the earth. Lucifer became Satan, the first sinner, and in continual rebellion against God. Satan hates God and all of God's creation. Once Satan saw God create Adam and Eve, Satan sought to destroy them. Satan came to Eve and tempted her to disobey God, just like Satan had. He told her she could be like God. He told her she could decide for herself what was good and evil instead of having to listen to God. Satan told her God was holding back something good from her.

> **Now the serpent was more cunning than any beast of the field which the Lord God had made. And he said to the woman, "Has God indeed said, 'You shall not eat of every tree of the garden'?" And the woman said to the serpent, "We may eat the fruit of the trees of the garden; but of the fruit of the tree which is in the**

midst of the garden, God has said, 'You shall not eat it, nor shall you touch it, lest you die.'" Then the serpent said to the woman, "You will not surely die. For God knows that in the day you eat of it your eyes will be opened, and you will be like God, knowing good and evil." (Genesis 3:1-5)(NKJV)

What had God told Adam to do before Satan came to tempt Eve?

Then the Lord God took the man and put him in the garden of Eden to tend and keep it. (Genesis 2:15)(NKJV)

God told Adam to "tend and keep" the garden. The Hebrew word translated "keep" means "guard and protect." God's will was that Adam would exercise dominion over all the creatures on the earth. All the creatures included Satan and any animal Satan would use to speak to Adam or Eve. God's stated will was that Adam would "guard and protect" the Garden of Eden from all unwelcome intruders. Did Adam do what God told him to do? Did Adam exercise his authority over Satan to keep him out of the garden? Did Adam cooperate with God by refusing to eat of the fruit from the tree of the knowledge of good and evil? The answer is "No," on all three counts.

> **So when the woman saw that the tree was good for food, that it was pleasant to the eyes, and a tree desirable to make one wise, she took of its fruit and ate. She also gave to her husband with her, and he ate. (Genesis 3:6)(NKJV)**

Where was Adam when Satan entered the Garden of Eden and talked to his wife, Eve? The Bible says Adam was "with her." Apparently, Adam stood right next to his wife and let Satan come into the garden and lie to Eve! Did Adam cooperate with God by guarding and protecting the Garden of Eden? No, he did not.

Was it God's will for Satan to enter the Garden of Eden? No, it wasn't. Was it God's will for Adam and

Eve to eat of the fruit of the tree of the knowledge of good and evil? It was absolutely not God's will. But isn't God sovereign? Yes, God is sovereign, but He also has bound Himself by His Word. When He gave the earth to His creation, Adam and Eve, He also created a boundary for Himself. He told Adam and Eve they were in charge of the earth. They had the responsibility to run their lives. They had the choice to cooperate with God to see His will come to pass or to act outside of the will of God. God would not cross the boundary He had set for Himself when He gave the earth to mankind.

Did you notice that God didn't come down to the Garden and run Satan off? God also didn't grab Adam's arm to keep him from eating the forbidden fruit. Why didn't He? Was it God's plan for Satan to lie to Eve? Was it God's plan for Adam to sin? Was it God's plan for the earth to be cursed because of sin? No! No! No! None of those things was God's will. Yet they happened without God lifting a finger to stop it.

God works according to His Word. His ways and thoughts are revealed through His written Word, which we call the Bible. He cannot work in violation of His own Word without becoming a liar. God has to play by His own rules. Since God cannot lie, we can depend on His Word to always be true.

> "My thoughts are nothing like your thoughts," says the Lord. "And my ways are far beyond anything you could imagine. For just as the heavens are higher than the earth, so my ways are higher than your ways and my thoughts higher than your thoughts. "The rain and snow come down from the heavens and stay on the ground to water the earth. They cause the grain to grow, producing seed for the farmer and bread for the hungry. It is the same with my word. I send it out, and it always produces fruit. It will accomplish all I want it to, and it will prosper everywhere I send it. (Isaiah 55:8-11)

God sent His ways and thoughts down to us in the form of His word, the Bible. God's sovereignty has to be understood in relation to His revealed will. His will is found in His written Word. It was God's sovereign will to give mankind a free will. God chose to give us the opportunity to work **with** Him or **against** Him. If we are proud and refuse to cooperate with Him, He resists us and provides no help. A proud person says, "I can handle everything on my own." "I have all the answers." "I am strong enough to deal with anything that comes my way." However, if we humble ourselves and cooperate with God, He makes His power and ability available to us freely as an act of His grace. A humble person says, "I need help." "I can't handle life on my own." "I admit I have weaknesses and I need someone to help me."

> **Likewise you younger people, submit yourselves to your elders. Yes, all of you be submissive to one another, and be clothed with humility, for "God resists the proud, But gives grace to the humble." (1 Peter 5:5) (NKJV)**

Decisions

People can make good decisions by cooperating with God. Good decisions bring good results. People can also make bad decisions. Bad decisions produce bad consequences. A drunk driver crashing into another car and killing an entire family is the result of a bad decision to drive drunk, not the plan of God. A child who is sexually molested is the result of a demon-controlled pedophile, not the plan of God. God gives all of us a free will. You can cooperate with God or you can cooperate with God's adversary, the devil. You can put this book down and go rob a convenience store and God will not stop you. You can make that choice, but don't tell the store owner it was all part of God's plan for his life.

Evidence Is Required

In America, evidence is required before a person can be held accountable for a crime. Anyone can accuse anyone of committing a criminal act. However, a person cannot be convicted unless enough evidence is presented to prove the person is guilty of the crime with which they have been charged.

Some people accuse God of acts for which there is no evidence to prove His guilt. When people face tragedies they often ask the question, "Why did God allow this to happen?" The answer many give is, "Everything happens for a reason." "We don't understand it, but it must have been part of God's plan since He allowed it to happen." People blame God for hurricanes, tornadoes, birth defects, sickness, accidents and other tragedies. But is there any evidence to prove these claims? Or are there only assumptions?

We do not live in Heaven. There is no corruption and there is no adversary in Heaven. An adversary is one who is opposed to your course of action. We have an adversary in this world. His name is Satan. He hates God and he hates you. His desire is to disrupt God's plans as much as possible. Satan wants to cause as much suffering as he can. He looks for people he can harass and influence. There is coming a day appointed by God when Satan will be cast into the lake of fire to be tormented forever. However, until that time comes, he has a right to be on this earth and to oppose God and God's family. Much of the suffering in the world today is because of the activity of Satan and his demonic forces of darkness.

> **Be sober, be vigilant; because your adversary the devil walks about like a roaring lion, seeking whom he may devour. Resist him, steadfast in the faith, knowing that the same sufferings are experienced by your brotherhood in the world. (1 Peter 5:8-9)(NKJV)**

This world is not functioning according to God's original plan. There were no tornado sirens in the Garden of Eden. There were no snake bite kits or cancer treatment centers. God's original creation has been corrupted. It was corrupted when Adam sinned and it will not be totally corrected until God replaces it with a new Heaven and a new earth. All of God's creation yearns for that final redemption when the curse due to sin is lifted.

> **Yet what we suffer now is nothing compared to the glory he will reveal to us later. For all creation is waiting eagerly for that future day when God will reveal who his children really are. Against its will, all creation was subjected to God's curse. But with eager hope, the creation looks forward to the day when it will join God's children in glorious freedom from death and decay. For we know that all creation has been groaning as in the pains of childbirth right up to the present time. And we believers also groan, even though we have the Holy Spirit within us as a foretaste of future glory, for we long for our bodies to be released from sin and suffering. We, too, wait with eager hope for the day when God will give us our full rights as his adopted children, including the new bodies he has promised us. (Romans 8:18–23)**

Your body is not totally redeemed yet, is it? Your body is corruptible, subject to sickness, decay and death. You get tired and need to sleep. You must feed your body for it to function properly. One day your body will be totally redeemed. You will no longer have to eat to stay strong. You won't have to sleep to refresh yourself. One day you will no longer have to resist sickness and disease because it will be eliminated from the earth. Have you ever been totally worn out, hungry, battling sickness and thought about how one day you won't have to deal with all this? You eagerly look forward to that wonderful day, but you know that day is not here yet. The earth is the same way. God's creation operates under a curse because of the sin of Adam. The earth "groans," looking forward to the day the curse is lifted.

The curse of sin on the earth is a reason we have tornadoes, earthquakes, floods, hurricanes, droughts and other natural disasters. We can't blame all those things on God. Adam's sin brought a curse on the earth. Is there any evidence that God sends tornadoes to destroy schools and homes and kill innocent children? Is there any evidence to prove God sends earthquakes which destroy businesses and cause people to be crushed to death? Can anyone prove God is the reason for these things? Disasters will continue to occur because the earth is cursed and corrupted, not because they are part of God's plan for our lives.

Many people get caught up in trying to understand everything that happens in life. Did God cause this or did Satan cause it? Maybe neither one! If God hasn't revealed the answer in the Bible, and He hasn't told you the answer personally, maybe you shouldn't be concerned about it. God is under no obligation to explain every event on this earth to you and me. He has the right to reveal what He chooses and to leave some things a mystery.

> **"The Lord our God has secrets known to no one. We are not accountable for them, but we and our children are accountable forever for all that he has revealed to us, so that we may obey all the terms of these instructions."**
> **(Deuteronomy 29:29)**

OUR RESPONSIBILITY IS TO ALIGN OURSELVES WITH GOD AND COOPERATE WITH HIM AT ALL TIMES SO WE WON'T BE THE REASON FOR OUR PROBLEMS.

God wants to help us. However, in many cases, He has done all He can do. We stand like Moses facing the Red Sea. We face an obstacle that God can help us overcome, but deliverance requires action on our part. My prayer is that God will use this book to help you see how to cooperate with God to see life-changing results.

2. SALVATION

THE BEST PLACE TO START TO ILLUSTRATE THE principle of cooperating with God is with the salvation experience. What is the will of God concerning people being saved from the penalty for sin?

> **The Lord isn't really being slow about his promise, as some people think. No, he is being patient for your sake. He does not want anyone to be destroyed, but wants everyone to repent. (2 Peter 3:9)**

God doesn't want anyone to be separated from Him forever. He wants everybody to be saved from eternal condemnation and punishment. Is everybody saved? Of course not. Since everybody in the world is not saved, then God's will doesn't automatically come to pass because He is sovereign. Every individual has a part to play in being saved. People cannot be saved until they learn to cooperate with God. God has His part to play and we have our part.

Recently, I noticed I had accidentally brushed against my car bumper and had a dirt streak on my pants. It wasn't something I did on purpose. It was an accident. You can't be born again by accident. You can't tell someone, "I think I might have gotten saved last night. I didn't mean to. It wasn't something I intended to do. It just happened accidentally." That is just not the way it works.

So what do we have to do to cooperate with God for salvation? Many people have interesting ideas about the answer to that question. The only ideas that count with God, though, are found in the Bible. Some think that doing good works will earn them a place in heaven. The Barna Group[1] lists this amazing statistic: Over half the people (54 percent) in

---

1 **The Barna Group 2005, Ventura, CA**

America believe that, "if a person is generally good, or does enough good things for others during their lives, they will earn a place in heaven." Will there be a huge scale at heaven's gate? Will God put all our good works on one side and all our bad works on the other side to determine if we can get into heaven? Apparently many believe the determining factor is to have at least one more good work than bad works and you can slide in. Is that how we cooperate with God for salvation; by doing good works?

> **God saved you by his grace when you believed. And you can't take credit for this; it is a gift from God. Salvation is not a reward for the good things we have done, so none of us can boast about it. (Ephesians 2:8-9)**

The Bible is clear that salvation is a gift from God. We cannot boast of earning our entrance into heaven. No one can stand before God and plead his case based on teaching a Sunday school class or giving money to the poor or being faithful to his spouse.

People cannot say they earned their way in because they were as good as their neighbor and never did a big sin like murder. Boasting about your good works is not the way to cooperate with God for salvation.

Repent

Jesus told us what to do.

> Later on, after John was arrested, Jesus went into Galilee, where he preached God's Good News. "The time promised by God has come at last!" he announced. "The Kingdom of God is near! Repent of your sins and believe the Good News!" (Mark 1:14–15)

And Peter preached the same message.

> Now repent of your sins and turn to God, so that your sins may be wiped away. (Acts 3:19)

The first thing to do is to repent. Repent means to think differently, to turn and go a different direction. Repent means turning away from sin. It also means turning away from keeping a religious system of do's and don'ts or rules and regulations which you thought would earn favor with God for salvation. And it means turning away from your own ideas about how to satisfy God and earn your salvation. God cannot repent for you. That is not His part. The only person who can repent as a step in your salvation is you.

BELIEVE

The second thing Jesus said to do is believe the gospel. The word, "gospel" means good news. The good news is that salvation is available free of charge as a gift. Sin brings death, or separation from God, but Jesus brings reconciliation.

> **For the wages of sin is death, but the free gift of God is eternal life through Christ Jesus our Lord. (Romans 6:23)**

But what does it mean to "believe?" Does that mean we only have to believe in God? Or to just believe that Jesus existed? Does it mean we only have to believe that Jesus was crucified on a cross? Most people believe in God. But that isn't enough. Even Satan and his demons believe in God.

You say you have faith, for you believe that there is one God. Good for you! Even the demons believe this, and they tremble in terror. (James 2:19)

Just believing in the existence of God and Jesus will not bring salvation. Another step is required to cooperate with God for salvation. I grew up going to church. My mother played the piano at the church in my hometown. I sat on the front pew in front of the piano and listened to sermon after sermon. At the conclusion of every service I had the opportunity to respond to that message about Jesus. I heard the gospel message. I believed in God. I believed that Jesus died for the sins of the world. But I still wasn't saved. I wasn't saved because I had not made it personal. I had not put my faith in Jesus.

> **So then faith comes by hearing, and hearing by the word of God. (Romans 10:17) (NKJV)**

The Greek word translated "word" in the Scripture above is "rhema." It means, "a spoken word or utterance." A "rhema" is a word from God spoken to you personally. I remember sitting in class in high school listening to the teacher. He was talking to everybody in the class, which included me. But my mind wandered at times until he called my name and said, "Randy, I want you to work this problem on the board." All of a sudden his word took on special meaning. He wasn't just talking to the whole class, he was talking to me.

God's word will have no effect on you until you receive it as a message spoken to you personally. It has to move from God talking to the whole world to God talking to you. When that happens, then faith comes into your heart and what you have believed comes to pass. In the Old Testament, God gave a promise to the Israelites. He told them after Moses delivered them from the bondage of slavery in Egypt that they could move to a new land called Canaan. God told them to drive out the inhabitants of the land because He would be with them and cause them to be victorious. But when they arrived at the border to Canaan all but two people refused to go in! They were afraid. They did not believe God's word about protecting them and giving them victory. The word of God did them no good because they did not take it personally. They did not believe. And because they did not believe, the word of God did not produce faith in them.

> For who, having heard, rebelled? Indeed, was it not all who came out of Egypt, led by Moses? Now with whom was He angry forty years? Was it not with those who sinned, whose corpses fell in the wilderness? And to whom did He swear that they would not en-

ter His rest, but to those who did not obey? So we see that they could not enter in because of unbelief. Therefore, since a promise remains of entering His rest, let us fear lest any of you seem to have come short of it. For indeed the gospel was preached to us as well as to them; but the word which they heard did not profit them, not being mixed with faith in those who heard it. (Hebrews 3:16-4:2)(NKJV)

One night during a church service I heard the gospel message. I heard that we were all sinners and that Jesus died to pay for the sins of the world. It was the same message I had heard many times before. But something changed inside me. I suddenly realized that I was a sinner. I realized that I needed a savior. I realized that Jesus didn't just die for the sins of the world, He died for my sins. The word of God had become a word personally spoken to me. Faith arose in my heart and I made a decision to trust Jesus for my salvation. I called on the name of the Lord because I needed a personal savior.

> **For "Everyone who calls on the name of the Lord will be saved." (Romans 10:13)**

I could not be saved until I cooperated with God. I had to turn away from sin, good works, pride in my own goodness, anything that kept me from God. I had to humble myself before God and admit I needed His help. When I did my part of repentance, humbling myself and trusting Jesus totally to make me righteous, then God did His part and caused me to be born again. God's will wasn't accomplished until I cooperated with Him.

3. Guidance

If I had to rank the top three prayer requests I receive, guidance for decisions would definitely be on that list. Most Christians sincerely want to discern God's will. The easy answer to questions about godly guidance is to say, "Read the Bible and follow the principles you find there." That is a good answer, but it does not provide the help for which most people are asking. The Bible is definitely the first place to start when seeking God's direction for your life. However, there are many decisions we have to make which the Bible cannot answer. Answers to questions like, "Who should I marry?" "What vocation should I pursue?" "Where should I live?" "What house should I buy?"

Do you think God is interested in helping us with those decisions? Two extreme positions can be taken on the subject of divine guidance. One extreme says when the Holy Spirit finished writing the Bible by inspiring its authors, His work was finished. Those who take this position say the only divine guidance available is through the written words in the Bible. They say we should follow the general principles found there, and as long as we don't violate the written Word of God, we are in the will of God.

The other extreme says we should not take any action or make any decisions until we have heard God's specific direction. Making a move without hearing from God is a good way to get outside the will of God. God is providing direction at all times; we just have to tune in to hear it.

The first position doesn't seem to line up with the Bible because of the Scriptures I will share with you shortly. The second is an ideal position of spiritual maturity which we should all strive to attain. However, most of us don't have our spiritual receivers fine-tuned to hear the Holy Spirit immediately for every decision we face. What should we do then? We should continue to develop a close relationship with God so we can become accustomed to hearing and recognizing His voice. But while we are on the journey to reach that ideal position, we can learn to cooperate with God to recognize His guidance in other ways.

Is there Scriptural evidence to prove we are supposed to receive God's guidance beyond the written Bible? And if so, how do we recognize His leading? The first step is to understand the human spirit and how God created man. John 4:24 says, *"For God is Spirit, so those who worship him must worship in spirit and in truth."* The spirit is the eternal part of us created in God's image.

> **Then the Lord God formed the man from the dust of the ground. He breathed the breath of life into the man's nostrils, and the man became a living person. (Genesis 2:7)**

God **formed** man's body out of the chemicals and substances He had already created in the earth. But then He **breathed** into man and created the eternal spirit. Animals had a "breath of life," but God personally breathed His breath, His eternal being, into man and created his eternal spirit. Some people believe when the physical body dies that the person ceases to exist. But that is not true. In Genesis 1:26–27 God said *"...Let us make human beings in our image, to be like us....So God created human beings in his own image. In the image of God he created them; male and female he created them."*

God is eternal. We are created in His image so we are also eternal beings. Our bodies aren't eternal, but our spirits are. The human spirit leaves the body at the time of physical death. But it continues to exist for eternity either in the presence of God or separated from God in torment.

The spirit of a man is the lamp of the Lord, Searching all the inner depths of his heart. (Proverbs 20:27)(NKJV)

The spirit of a man or woman is where God shines His light of revelation. When I was growing up, my family had a cabin on the Illinois River in northeastern Oklahoma. I always took a big flashlight with me on weekends we would spend there. After dark, the flashlight showed me the path I was to walk. God, who **is** Spirit, communicates with **our** spirits. That is what Jesus told us the Holy Spirit would do.

> **And I will ask the Father, and he will give you another Advocate, who will never leave you. He is the Holy Spirit, who leads into all truth. The world cannot receive him, because it isn't looking for him and doesn't recognize him. But you know him, because he lives with you now and later will be in you. (John 14:16-17)**

Jesus said after He completed His work on the earth and ascended to the Father He would send back the Holy Spirit. He said the Holy Spirit would not just be **with** us, but would live **inside** believers. This is great news! We no longer have to go to a temple to find the presence of God.

> **Don't you realize that all of you together are the temple of God and that the Spirit of God lives in you? (1 Corinthians 3:16)**

Every person who has turned away from sin and trusted Jesus for salvation has been born again and has the Holy Spirit living inside.

> **But you are not controlled by your sinful nature. You are controlled by the Spirit if you have the Spirit of God living in you. (And remember that those who do not have the Spirit of Christ living in them do not belong to him at all.) (Romans 8:9)**

Now that we have the Holy Spirit living inside of us we should learn to discern the leading of the Holy Spirit.

> **For all who are led by the Spirit of God are children of God. (Romans 8:14)**

Notice that we are to be "led" by the Holy Spirit. That can mean different things at different times in our lives. I had a toy dachshund named Pepper when I was a child. I never did accomplish much when I tried to train that dog. If he got out the front door, he would run wild in the neighborhood. I could call his name for hours, but he paid no attention to what I said. This was a game to him.

The only way I could control Pepper was with a leash. If I had a leash around his neck, I could lead him wherever I wanted him to go. Other pet owners have trained their pets to obey their spoken word. When they say "sit," the dog sits. When they say "here," the dog comes running. They get their pet where they want it by the spoken word while I got mine to go where I wanted by a leash. Does it really matter which method is used as long as the pet gets where you want it?

Ideally, we will hear the gentle voice of the Holy Spirit within us telling us what to do. The reality for most of us is that we don't always hear that voice as clearly as we would like. We like to share about the times we have heard His direction clearly. But there are plenty of times we have not heard a clear word from the Holy Spirit. So maybe God still wants to "lead" us even though He would prefer we hear and obey His spoken Word. God can lead us if we will cooperate with Him.

ONE STEP AT A TIME

If I want to talk to my neighbor, I have to walk across the street to get to his house. I can't jump from my front door to his yard. I can only get there by taking a series of steps. A series of steps starts with the first step. God leads us in steps. He doesn't usually jump us from one point to the next. He leads us one step at a time.

> **The Lord directs the steps of the godly. He delights in every detail of their lives. (Psalm 37:23)**

I don't like surprises. I like to be in control of my life. When I take a trip, I look at the map to see where I am going before I start. I want to know what highways to take each leg of the trip. I make hotel reservations before I leave. I plan out how long it will take to drive to the first night's stop and what time I need to leave the following morning. I like to have all the details worked out before I leave home. God doesn't always give us that kind of information when He is leading us. He told Abram (Genesis 12:1) to leave his homeland and family and "*...go to the land that I will show you.*" I would not have liked that kind of directive. I would have wanted to know where I was going before I left. If we are going to serve God, however, we have to be willing to play by His rules. He is under no obligation to show us the end of a journey and all the stops along the way before we begin.

> **Trust in the Lord with all your heart; do not depend on your own understanding. Seek his will in all you do, and he will show you which path to take. (Proverbs 3:5-6)**

God knows the pathway on which He leads us. He knows where it will end up and He knows the obstacles we will encounter along the way. We have to be willing to cooperate with God and start down the path He is leading us even though we don't know how long the journey will be or where it will end.

I lived in Montgomery, Alabama, for 12 years. Interstate 65 runs through Montgomery and north to Birmingham, 90 miles away. The straightest route to Birmingham is on I-65. Let's assume I want to drive from Montgomery to Birmingham at night so I park my car facing north in the right-hand lane of I-65. Let's also assume an Alabama trooper pulls in behind me, walks up to my car and asks me what I am doing.

"I need to go to Birmingham," I say.

The trooper replies, "Well, just drive north on this Interstate and you will be there in about 90 minutes."

"Oh no!" I say. "I'm not leaving until I can see the city of Birmingham with my headlights."

You know what that trooper would do next? He would be on his radio calling for backup to assist him with a crazy driver parked on the Interstate highway! <u>If I wait until I see my destination, I will never leave</u>. My headlights show the path directly ahead of me. The only way to see farther down the road is to start driving. I have to trust that the state highway department has put up signs that tell me when I have reached Birmingham. I will know when to exit because the signs will be lighted to show me the way I need to go.

God may not tell you when or where your journey will end. You may only have an urgency in your spirit to go a certain direction. If so, God is **leading** you. It may not be the spoken word you would prefer, but it is still His leading. Your part of this process of cooperating with God is to **start** to move in the direction He is leading you.

I graduated from Oklahoma State University with an engineering degree. Three years later I was working as a consulting engineer when God began to put a desire in my heart to go to Bible school. That is all He showed me. He didn't explain what I would do after graduating from Bible school. He didn't show me where I would be in 20 years. He only prompted me to leave my engineering job and go to Bible school. I obeyed the inner leading. That was the first step in a number of seasons of development in my life. What if I had said, "God, I am not leaving my engineering career until you show me everything you have planned for me for the next 20 years?" I would probably still be working as an engineer. I would have missed God's plan if I insisted on seeing the end of the journey before I began.

Some of you may be thinking, "But what if I make a wrong move?" Or, "What if I do something that turns out to not be His leading?"

Your Holy Spirit Alarm

When I was in college, and for a few years afterward, I worked as a baseball umpire. I positioned myself behind the catcher so I could have the best view of the ball crossing home plate. I decided if the pitch was a strike or ball. If a runner tried to score, I called the runner safe or out. When the ball was hit, I let the players know if it was fair or foul. My job as an umpire was to make the calls. God has given every believer an umpire to make the calls in your spirit.

> **And let the peace that comes from Christ rule in your hearts. For as members of one body you are called to live in peace. And always be thankful. (Colossians 3:15)**

The root of the Greek word translated "rule" means "umpire." The verse above could be translated, *"Let the peace of God be the umpire in your hearts..."* Remember, the umpire makes the call. He decides if you are fair or foul. The peace of God in your heart lets you know you are **in** the will of God. The lack of peace in your heart is an indication you are **out** of the will of God. Look at that verse in the Amplified translation.

> **And let the peace (soul harmony which comes) from Christ rule (act as umpire continually) in your hearts [deciding and set-**

tling with finality all questions that arise in your minds, in that peaceful state] to which as [members of Christ's] one body you were also called [to live]. And be thankful (appreciative), [giving praise to God always]. (Colossians 3:15)(Amp)

We purchased a house in 1992 which was equipped with a burglar alarm system. It included an outdoor and indoor siren that sounded when the alarm was triggered. We moved into the house over several days instead of doing it all in one day.

One night I went to the house after dark to move some things in. The back door lock broke when I put the key in so I was not able to open that door. The front entrance had an exterior glass storm door which was locked from the inside. My only option to enter was a side door which opened into the laundry room. I knew I would only have 20 seconds to deactivate the alarm once the door opened.

I unlocked the side door, stepped in and was confronted with another door between the laundry room and the kitchen. That door was locked and I did not have a key to open it. Twenty seconds later the powerful alarm siren pierced the night air of this quiet neighborhood. I ran back around to the front of the house expecting to see neighbors coming out to investigate the commotion. Only one elderly couple peered out their front door to see what was happening. I waved at them and they went back inside.

That wasn't what I expected. When my house alarm goes off, I want to see the entire neighborhood outside immediately with rifles and pistols loaded and pointed at my house! The alarm is a signal that **someone is where they shouldn't be.**

You have a Holy Spirit alarm inside of you waiting to go off if you step outside God's will. Instead of being afraid to make a move, take a step! Start down a path if you believe God is leading you. Trust God enough to know He will set off an alarm in your spirit if you have made the wrong move. If you are going to live by faith, you have to be willing to make a mistake. God will forgive you if you take a wrong step. Then He will help you get back on track.

A number of years ago I was looking for a new car. My wife and I had decided what kind of car we wanted. The only decisions left were which dealership to buy it from and how much to pay. I drove into a dealership one day and asked to see the type of car we had decided on. They had one, and I test-drove it. All the time I was driving that car there was tremendous turmoil inside my spirit. It got worse after we went back into the sales office to discuss a price. I made a ridiculously low offer so I could leave as soon as possible.

The manager came in and told me how much he wanted to sell me the car. The turmoil wouldn't go away. My alarm was going off! I was somewhere I wasn't supposed to be! I told them I couldn't buy the car and left immediately. My insides were still churning as I drove away from the dealership. I cried out to God, "Okay, I won't buy the car there. Please leave me alone!"

God had protected me from making the wrong decision. The lack of peace in my spirit made the call that I was in the wrong place. We eventually were led by God's peace in our spirits to purchase a car from another dealership. That car served us for well over 100,000 miles.

Paul had to deal with a similar situation. He and his ministry team were busy preaching the gospel everywhere they could. But the Holy Spirit began to help channel his efforts.

> Next Paul and Silas traveled through the area of Phrygia and Galatia, because the Holy Spirit had prevented them from preaching the word in the province of Asia at that time. Then coming to the borders of Mysia, they headed north for the province of Bithynia, but again the Spirit of Jesus did not allow them to go there. So instead, they went on through Mysia to the seaport of Troas. That night Paul had a vision: A man from Macedonia in northern Greece was standing there, pleading with him, "Come over to Macedonia and help us!" So we decided to leave for Macedonia at once, having concluded that God was calling us to preach the Good News there. (Acts 16:6–10)

Paul was on the move. He wasn't afraid to start. He didn't sit at home fasting and praying for a month before he would preach the gospel. His job was to preach, and he was preaching. But the Holy Spirit stopped him from going the wrong direction twice. He started to go to Asia and the Holy Spirit said, "No." He tried to head to Bithynia, but the Holy Spirit said, "No." Then the Holy Spirit made it clear He wanted Paul to go to Macedonia.

God can direct your efforts more easily when you are on the move. Have you ever tried to turn the wheel of a parked car? It is very hard to do. But if you start the car moving, even just a little bit, it is easy to turn the wheel and guide the car where you want it to go.

Samuel was a prophet of God in Old Testament times. Saul, the current king, had disobeyed God one too many times. God decided to prepare a replacement for Saul. God spoke to Samuel about anointing a new king for the nation of Israel. Samuel was upset because he had anointed Saul to be king many years earlier and he did not want to see him fail. But God had made His decision.

> Now the Lord said to Samuel, "You have mourned long enough for Saul. I have rejected him as king of Israel, so fill your flask with olive oil and go to Bethlehem. Find a man named Jesse who lives there, for I have selected one of his sons to be my king." (1 Samuel 16:1)

Jesse had eight sons. Did you notice God didn't tell him which son to anoint? Samuel had to cooperate with God for God's will to be accomplished. Jesse had seven of his sons at home when Samuel arrived. They each stood before Samuel as he prepared to anoint the new king.

> When they arrived, Samuel took one look at Eliab and thought, "Surely this is the Lord's anointed!" But the Lord said to Samuel, "Don't judge by his appearance or height, for I have rejected him. The Lord doesn't see things the way you see them. People judge by outward appearance, but the Lord looks at the heart." Then Jesse told his son Abinadab to step for-

ward and walk in front of Samuel. But Samuel said, "This is not the one the Lord has chosen." Next Jesse summoned Shimea, but Samuel said, "Neither is this the one the Lord has chosen." In the same way all seven of Jesse's sons were presented to Samuel. But Samuel said to Jesse, "The Lord has not chosen any of these." Then Samuel asked, "Are these all the sons you have?" "There is still the youngest," Jesse replied. "But he's out in the fields watching the sheep and goats." "Send for him at once," Samuel said. "We will not sit down to eat until he arrives." So Jesse sent for him. He was dark and handsome, with beautiful eyes. And the Lord said, "This is the one; anoint him." So as David stood there among his brothers, Samuel took the flask of olive oil he had brought and anointed David with the oil. And the Spirit of the Lord came powerfully upon David from that day on. Then Samuel returned to Ramah. (1 Samuel 16:6–13)

Samuel stood before seven of Jesse's sons one at a time. Every time God said, "No, he is not the one." Finally, they brought David, the youngest, out of the field and Samuel knew this was the one. Why didn't God just tell Samuel to go anoint Jesse's son, **David**, to be king? It sure would have simplified the process.

I believe this story shows us how God wants us to walk by faith. He wants us to trust Him to tell us what we need to know when we need to know it. Samuel didn't find out which son to anoint king until he had obeyed God by going to Jesse's home. Samuel had to cooperate with God before His will could be totally revealed.

The ideal situation is that we hear specific direction from God on what to do when we face a decision. When you hear a specific word in your spirit, by all means obey Him and do what He says. However, if you are not hearing clearly, cooperate with God by making a move in the direction you feel led. Trust Him to let you know if you have made, or are about to make, the wrong move. And trust Him to give you further direction when you need it.

4. Answered Prayer

Thousands of books have been written about prayer. Theologians have studied the subject from every angle imaginable. I make no pretense that this chapter describes the only aspects we need to be concerned with concerning prayer. This is only part of the answer to consistent, answered prayer. It is a part many have overlooked because of traditional thinking about the proper way to approach God. Let's look at how can we cooperate with God to see results in our prayer life.

Pray

If you believe the extreme teaching of God's sovereignty, you would say there is no need to pray.

Some would say we should simply live our lives with an ongoing trust that God will cause the things He wants to happen. Why spend time praying if God is going to do whatever He wants because He is "sovereign?" The truth is that we have a part to play in bringing God's will into the earth. Everything doesn't always happen just because God wants it to. The prayers of believers are essential to open the door for God to move and manifest Himself in the affairs of mankind.

Jesus was a man with a consistent prayer life. It must have been obvious to His disciples that prayer was an important part of His lifestyle. Jesus' disciples saw the way God moved in His life so they asked Jesus to teach them how to pray. Jesus answered by giving them a model prayer. He did not tell them to pray this prayer word for word, but His response gave them some principles to follow. Part of that prayer has to do with praying God's will into the earth. This is what Jesus said:

In this manner, therefore, pray: Our Father in heaven, Hallowed be Your name. Your king-

dom come. Your will be done on earth as it is in heaven. Give us this day our daily bread. And forgive us our debts, as we forgive our debtors. And do not lead us into temptation, but deliver us from the evil one. For Yours is the kingdom and the power and the glory forever. Amen. (Matthew 6:9-13)(NKJV)

Jesus said to pray for God's kingdom to be established and God's will to be done. Why would He tell them to pray about those things if God is "sovereign" and will do what He wants anyway? Why did Jesus pray so much that His disciples took note of it if God's "sovereignty" ruled the earth? Because we have a part to play. The Bible contains many examples of God requiring, even asking, people to pray so He can respond and do what He wants to do. In fact, Jesus talked about the importance of continued, persistent prayer. He made it clear that God will only respond <u>after</u> we do our part.

"Keep on asking, and you will receive what you ask for. Keep on seeking, and you will find.

> **Keep on knocking, and the door will be opened to you. For everyone who asks, receives. Everyone who seeks, finds. And to everyone who knocks, the door will be opened. (Matthew 7:7-8)**

All three of these actions produce results. The "receiving, finding and opening" results only occur after you do your part. You will not receive unless you "ask." You will not find what you are looking for unless you "seek" or look for it. The door will not open on its own; you have to "knock" on it first. James 4:2 says something very similar, *"Yet you don't have what you want because you don't ask God for it."*

BE SPECIFIC

One way to cooperate with God is to ask Him for what we want. Now some of you are saying, "I already know that." Yet many people make the mistake of forgetting to tell God exactly what they want or need. It is easy to get caught up in telling Him all about our problems and forgetting to make a specific request.

Imagine a mother stumbling into a restaurant with two small children in tow and her arms full of packages. She sits down at a table and a waitress comes over and says, "What can I get for you today?" The woman responds, "You can't imagine what a day I have had! My little girl kept me up half the night coughing. I finally got in to see the doctor and he said she has an infection. We had to wait over an hour at the pharmacy to get the prescription filled. After that we headed to the shoe store to get new shoes for her and my son. We found some shoes we liked but they didn't have them in the right size. The next store we went to had the right sizes but the wrong colors. I couldn't make it another step until I got something to eat, so here we are."

The waitress smiles and says, "It sounds like you have had a rough day. What can I get for you?"

The woman launches into another tirade. "It's only going to get worse! My sister-in-law is coming in today to stay for the weekend and she will have her two kids with her. She's crazy as a loon and I don't even want her in my house..."

The waitress is ready to help the woman. She wants to help the woman. But why can't she help her? Because the woman has spent all her time talking about her problems instead of telling the waitress what she wants to eat! It is fine to talk to God about your problems. You should feel comfortable sharing your challenges with God. But at some point you will have to make a specific request if you want God to help you.

> **Don't worry about anything; instead, pray about everything. <u>Tell God what you need</u>, and thank him for all he has done. Then you will experience God's peace, which exceeds anything we can understand. His peace will guard your hearts and minds as you live in Christ Jesus. (Philippians 4:6–7)**

Did you notice that we are admonished not to "worry about anything?" If you don't worry about "anything," how many things does that leave to worry about? Worry and anxiety comes from dwelling on the problem instead of the answer. In order to cooperate with God, you have to tell him specifically what you need and then refuse to worry about it anymore. Telling God what you need requires you to define a specific request. Once you make your specific request, you can enjoy relief from stress and anxiety. Your heart and mind can be free from worry. You can have peace inside of you even though it makes no sense to your natural mind to have peace. You can be confident that God is answering your prayer if you prayed according to His will and made a specific request.

Praying With Confidence

Is there a way to pray which will guarantee success? Is it possible to say, "Amen" at the conclusion of prayer knowing that God heard and will grant our request? Or are we required to begin or end every prayer with the phrase, "if it be Thy will?"

> **And we are confident that he hears us whenever we ask for anything that pleases him. And since we know he hears us when we make our requests, we also know that he will give us what we ask for. (1 John 5:14–15)**

Confidence in God is a wonderful thing. Confidence means dependability. It means we can count on someone to come through for us. Do you know people in whom you have no confidence? Do you know people who tell you they will come by your house at 8:00 p.m. and you don't even turn on the porch light because you have no confidence in their word? I do. I also know people who are extremely dependable. I know I can depend on them to do what they say they will do. I have great confidence in them.

The Bible says there is a way to have confidence in God. There is a way to be confident that God will hear and answer your prayer. You can leave your time of prayer with great peace in your heart because you are confident God will help you and grant your prayer request. The way to have this confidence is to cooperate with God by praying for things we know would please Him and are in line with His will.

I am sure most Christians want God's will to be manifested in their lives. One way many people try to accomplish this is by beginning or ending every prayer with "if it be Thy will." Their hearts are right, but is this the best way to accomplish that goal? Some people ask God for everything they can think of and finish their prayer with "if it be Thy will." They figure that will ensure that God will throw out every request which isn't His will and grant the ones which are His will. However, if you don't know whether or not you are praying God's will, you cannot be confident that your prayer will be answered.

> **And it is impossible to please God without faith. Anyone who wants to come to him must believe that God exists and that he rewards those who sincerely seek him. (Hebrews 11:6)**

God wants us to use our faith. It pleases Him when we use our faith. He wants us to make using our faith an integral part of our lives. He said through the prophet in Habakkuk 2:4(NKJV), "*…the just shall live by his faith.*" Faith should not be something we only use in a time of crisis. Every day of our lives should be an exercise of our faith. But where does faith come from?

So then faith comes by hearing, and hearing by the word of God. (Romans 10:17) (NKJV)

Faith comes from the word of God. If we are going to live by faith, we will have to live by the word of God. God's will is expressed through His word. Faith in God, therefore, has to line up with the will of God. If we pray for something outside the will of God, there is no faith involved. Faith operates where the will of God is known. Faith comes from God's written word or from His words of specific direction revealed to our spirits.

His ways and thoughts are deep and full of revelation concerning His plans and purposes for our lives. The good news is that He has chosen to reveal His ways and thoughts to us through the written words in the Bible and through direct guidance from the Holy Spirit.

> "My thoughts are nothing like your thoughts," says the Lord. "And my ways are far beyond anything you could imagine. For just as the heavens are higher than the earth, so my ways are higher than your ways and my thoughts higher than your thoughts. "<u>The rain and snow come down from the heavens</u> and stay on the ground to water the earth. They cause the grain to grow, producing seed for the farmer and bread for the hungry. <u>It is the same with my word</u>. I send it out, and it always produces fruit. It will accomplish all I want it to, and it will prosper everywhere I send it. (Isaiah 55:8-11)

> **For all who are led by the Spirit of God are children of God. (Romans 8:14)**

God is not trying to hide His will from us. He does not want us to be in the dark about what He wants us to do. He inspired Paul to pray over the church members at Colosse that they would know the will of God. God has the same desire for every member of His church today.

> **So we have not stopped praying for you since we first heard about you. We ask God to give you complete knowledge of his will and to give you spiritual wisdom and understanding. (Colossians 1:9)**

God does not want His family members to be without wisdom concerning His plan for each of them.

> **Don't act thoughtlessly, but understand what the Lord wants you to do. (Ephesians 5:17)**

When we know God's will for our lives, we can pray accurately and confidently. We can pray in faith without wavering. Praying a multitude of requests with no idea of the will of God can cause you to waver. Wavering will keep your prayers from being answered. James was inspired by the Holy Spirit to write about praying in faith. He was specifically addressing praying for wisdom. However, no matter what you are praying for, the same faith principles apply.

If any of you lacks wisdom, let him ask of God, who gives to all liberally and without reproach, and it will be given to him. But let him ask in faith, with no doubting, for he who doubts is like a wave of the sea driven and tossed by the wind. For let not that man suppose that he will receive anything from the Lord; he is a double-minded man, unstable in all his ways. (James 1:5-8)(NKJV)

He said praying in faith means there can be no doubt. A person who doubts when he prays is like a wave on the sea. A wave can only respond to the wind and current. A wave is tossed back and forth. A person who doubts is tossed around by the circumstances of life. A person who doubts is double-minded. Double means "two." A double-minded person has two minds. One mind says what I am praying is God's will. The other mind says what I prayed is not God's will.

When the circumstances of life begin to look better, we assume God is answering our prayer. When things look worse, we assume we did not pray in line with God's will. Double-minded praying is praying with two minds. One mind says this is the will of God. One mind says this is not the will of God. A person like this is unstable and will not receive anything from the Lord.

The opposite of double-minded is single-minded. Single means "one." If we have one mind about prayer, it should be that we are praying in line with the will of God. Instead of praying for everything that comes to mind, we should take the time to find out what the will of God is before we pray. That way

4. Answered Prayer — 69

we can pray with confidence, knowing that God has heard and will answer our prayer.

The best way to insure that we are praying the will of God is to pray the Word of God. If we know we are praying His will, we know God will hear and answer that prayer. We can cooperate with God by searching His Word, the Bible, to find His promises before we pray. For example, if you need God's wisdom about a decision you have to make, you could phrase James 1:5 into a prayer like this:

"Father, you promised if I lacked wisdom I could come to you and you would give me your wisdom. You promised to give me your wisdom liberally and without reproaching me for not already knowing the answer. Father, please give me your wisdom about this decision. I am confident you have heard my prayer and are giving me your wisdom. Thank you for your help."

God wants to perform His Word. He is in a hurry to perform His Word. When we cooperate with Him by returning His Word to Him in prayer, it will not be void or without power.

Then the Lord said to me, "You have seen well, for I am ready to perform My word." (Jeremiah 1:12)(NKJV)

So shall My word be that goes forth from My mouth; It shall not return to Me void, But it shall accomplish what I please, And it shall prosper in the thing for which I sent it. (Isaiah 55:11)(NKJV)

5. Financial Provision

America is the most prosperous nation in the world. The standard of living for Americans far surpasses any other country. Unions will go on strike at the slightest mention of a reduction in salary or benefits. Some Americans will change jobs to make an extra 25 cents an hour. Money is an integral part of our lives. Yet, when Christian ministers preach that it is God's will for believers to be financially blessed, many begin to flinch.

"I don't want to hear that **prosperity gospel** around here!" some church members will proclaim.

"How can anyone think that God wants a person to be financially blessed?" some pastors argue.

The same people who make those arguments also usually want the nicest church building in town with extra padding on the pews and a state-of-the-art sound system. Those things all take money. Is it possible that God really is interested in the financial part of our lives? Is it possible we can cooperate with Him to see our financial needs met? Why would God want us to be blessed with money?

BLESSED TO BE A BLESSING

Thousands of years ago, God decided to make a covenant with a man named Abram. He told Abram He was going to bring great blessing to his life. God later changed Abram's name to Abraham. God also told Abram the purpose for his prosperity.

> **I will make you a great nation; I will bless you and make your name great; and you shall be a blessing. (Genesis 12:2)(NKJV)**

Notice that God was blessing Abram so Abram could be a blessing. God did not want Abram to hoard his abundance to himself. He wanted Abram to be a blessing to others. He wanted Abram to be a conduit through whom His prosperity could flow to help many. Paul wrote about this same truth in one of his letters to the Corinthian believers.

> **And God will generously provide all you need. Then you will always have everything you need and plenty left over to share with others. (2 Corinthians 9:8)**

SEEK GOD, NOT PROSPERITY

Many people who oppose any mention of financial prosperity are concerned about a wrong attitude. The wrong attitude about money can certainly cause problems. Jesus made it clear where our priorities should lie.

> **No one can serve two masters. For you will hate one and love the other; you will be devoted to one and despise the other. You cannot serve both God and money. (Matthew 6:24)**

> **Seek the Kingdom of God above all else, and live righteously, and he will give you everything you need. (Matthew 6:33)**

Prosperity should be a by-product of seeking God. Prosperity should not be our goal. Jesus said to seek God **first** and **then** all the things we need will be added to us. When our priorities remain in order, we know where the blessings come from. Even though it is God's will to bless us financially, we still have a part to play. We can cooperate with God or we can go our own way and miss out on what we could have had.

TITHING

Oh, no! Here comes the boring part about tithing and giving! Is that what you think? If so, you don't understand what it means to cooperate with God. Remember, God's will doesn't automatically happen unless we do our part. One part of walking in God's abundant financial provision involves understanding and activating the tithe.

Tithing is a principle, not a law. We no longer live under the law God gave to Israel through Moses. Jesus fulfilled that law and redeemed us from the consequences of disobeying the law. Tithing was practiced long before God made it part of the law that Moses delivered to the nation of Israel. The tithe is simply a way to say to God, "I recognize that everything I have comes from you. You are the Most High God, the possessor of heaven and earth." The word "tithe" means one-tenth. When you tithe, you give a tenth of your income to God.

Under the Old Covenant, before Jesus entered the earth, the tithe was given to a priest. The priest was God's representative on the earth. For example, Abram gave a tenth of his increase to the priest Melchizedek after God had given him a great victory. Abram's nephew, Lot, had been captured by a confederation of kings who had conquered the cities of Sodom and Gomorrah. Lot and his family lived in Sodom. These kings had captured all the inhabitants and also took all the material possessions of the prisoners.

Abram took 318 of his own servants and attacked the armies of the confederation of kings. God gave Abram a great victory and enabled him to rescue Lot, his family and all the other inhabitants of the two cities. As Abram was returning from the victory with the kings of Sodom and Gomorrah, a priest by the name of Melchizedek met them.

> **And Melchizedek, the king of Salem and a priest of God Most High, brought Abram some bread and wine. Melchizedek blessed Abram with this blessing: "Blessed be Abram by God Most High, Creator of heaven and earth. And blessed be God Most High, who has defeated your enemies for you." Then Abram gave Melchizedek a tenth of all the goods he had recovered. (Genesis 14:18–20)**

Did you notice what Abram did? He gave the priest, God's representative, a tithe of all the plunder he had rescued from the hands of the wicked confederation of kings. Melchizedek made it clear it was God who had given Abram the victory and the spoils of the victory. Abram's response was to give God a tenth as recognition that He was his provider. There was no law of Moses yet. There were no commands to tithe. Abram did it because it is a **principle**, not a law.

Later on, God incorporated the **principle** of tithing into the law of Moses which governed the nation of Israel. The priests were then sustained by the tithes of the people. Israelites would bring a tenth of their grain, sheep, vegetables, or any other increase, and take it to the storehouse for the priests. In return for their cooperation, God would insure that their financial needs were met abundantly.

> **Bring all the tithes into the storehouse so there will be enough food in my Temple. If you do," says the Lord of Heaven's Armies, "I will open the windows of heaven for you. I will pour out a blessing so great you won't have enough room to take it in! Try it! Put me to the test! (Malachi 3:10)**

God challenged the people to try Him, or test Him. He is saying, "I want to do my part. Just cooperate with me and give me a chance to prove myself to you!"

NEW COVENANT TITHING

The New Covenant Jesus established does not require temple sacrifices to sustain the priests. We do, however, have pastors, or shepherds, who have been given the oversight of local church bodies. These pastors report to the Chief Shepherd, Jesus. Pastors and the local church are responsible for providing ministry services according to the New Covenant as described in the New Testament. If the tithe was only described as part of the law of Moses, we would no longer be expected to observe that requirement. But remember, the tithe is a **principle** and not a law. The principle of tithing as a way of recognizing God as the source of all our material blessings hasn't ended. So tithing continues even though there are no longer temples and priests to receive the tithe.

There are no instructions in the New Testament to stop the tithe. We have no specific instruction in the New Testament about where to bring the tithe. It seems, however, that your local church, where you are fed the Word of God regularly, is the logical place to bring your tithe. Tithing, giving a tenth of your increase to God through your local church, shows that you recognize God's goodness in giving you what you have.

10% OF WHAT?

Since the word "tithe" means ten percent, what is the 100 percent? Do I take ten percent of my gross earnings before taxes and living expenses? Or do I take ten percent of what remains after taxes? Or after taxes and house payment? Or after taxes, house payment and groceries? Or after taxes, house payment, groceries and retirement? Or after taxes, house payment, groceries, retirement and vacation savings?

You can make that determination since there are no detailed instructions recorded in the Bible. However, the principle of tithing is fully demonstrated when you give God the tenth **first**, instead of waiting to see if you have enough left over after you have spent your money on your own needs and desires. If you give God the tenth first, then He can bless and multiply the remaining 90 percent. If you spend your money on other things **first** and give God the tenth **last**, He has nothing left to multiply.

> **Honor the Lord with your possessions, And with the <u>firstfruits</u> of all your increase; So your barns will be filled with plenty, And your vats will overflow with new wine. (Proverbs 3:9-10)(NKJV)**

Once again, when we do our part and honor God with the tithe first, He promises to provide financial abundance. Our part is to tithe. His part is to provide an overflow of financial blessing.

Planting And Harvesting

When a seed is planted in the proper environment, it will eventually produce a harvest. This is another **principle** which God established after Noah left the ark following the great flood. Principles never die. They continue to work under all circumstances.

> As long as the earth remains, there will be planting and harvest, cold and heat, summer and winter, day and night." (Genesis 8:22)

The principle of "planting and harvest" applies to plants, but it is also a spiritual principle. Whatever we plant, or sow, will result in a harvest of the same thing. When you plant tomato seeds, you harvest tomatoes. When you plant sunflower seeds, you will grow sunflowers. If we plant criticism by being critical of others, we will harvest criticism ourselves. If we are merciful with others, we will reap mercy when we need it. Paul repeated this truth in his letter to the Galatians.

> Don't be misled—you cannot mock the justice of God. You will always harvest what you plant. Those who live only to satisfy their own sinful nature will harvest decay and death from that sinful nature. But those who live to please the Spirit will harvest everlasting life from the Spirit. (Galatians 6:7-8)

Jesus talked about this principle, too. He emphasized that multiplication is a part of the reaping process. You get back much more than you plant. If you plant one watermelon seed, you reap several watermelons with hundreds of seeds. This same multiplication principle is true with whatever we plant.

> You must be compassionate, just as your Father is compassionate. "Do not judge others, and you will not be judged. Do not condemn others, or it will all come back against you. Forgive others, and you will be forgiven. Give, and you will receive. Your gift will return to you in full—pressed down, shaken

5. Financial Provision — 83

together to make room for more, running over, and poured into your lap. The amount you give will determine the amount you get back." (Luke 6:36–38)

What a wonderful promise! Jesus said whatever we plant will be multiplied back to us. What if you don't plant anything? There can be no harvest if no seed is planted. God can only multiply a seed that has been sown. Seed stored in a barn will never produce a harvest. This principle applies to handling our money, too. Many people have this attitude, "I will give something to God when I get a little extra money." But Jesus said just the opposite in **Luke 6:38**, didn't He? Jesus said giving has to come **first** before He will provide the overflowing blessing. Our part is to **give**. **God's** part is to cause the multiplied return.

Jesus also said the measure we use to plant will be what determines the size of the harvest. If you plant the seeds from a small package of tomato seeds, you will have a small harvest. However, if you plant the seeds from a 50-pound bag, you will have a huge harvest. The harvest is dependent on the measure used to plant the seeds.

WHERE DO I GIVE?

If my tithe belongs to my home church, where else should I give when I want to give more than one tenth? One option is to give where there is a need. You can give to the poor. Or a family whose husband lost his job. Or to your local church. Or to missionaries. Or to ministries outside the local church. Or to disaster relief. Remember that you determine the size of your financial harvest by the amount of seed you plant. God is **limited** in the return He provides by the amount of money **you** plant into a need. Paul was inspired to write about this principle of giving money as you would plant a seed in the second letter to the Corinthians. The entire ninth chapter is about handling your money.

> Remember this—a farmer who plants only a few seeds will get a small crop. But the one

5. Financial Provision — 85

who plants generously will get a generous crop. (2 Corinthians 9:6)

Simon Peter was faced with an opportunity to give. Peter owned a fishing business. One of his business assets was a boat. Jesus needed his boat one day. A huge crowd had followed Jesus. He was confronted with a mass of people in front of Him and a lake behind Him. Jesus needed a way to be able to speak to the people so everyone could hear.

One day as Jesus was preaching on the shore of the Sea of Galilee, great crowds pressed in on him to listen to the word of God. He noticed two empty boats at the water's edge, for the fishermen had left them and were washing their nets. Stepping into one of the boats, Jesus asked Simon, its owner, to push it out into the water. So he sat in the boat and taught the crowds from there. (Luke 5:1-3)

Peter gave something to Jesus. Jesus taught a principle we already looked at in **Luke 6:38** about giving producing an abundant return. Peter's business was fishing. He gave the use of his fishing boat to Jesus. If Jesus' words are true about giving, than Simon Peter is in for a tremendous blessing!

> **When he had finished speaking, he said to Simon, "Now go out where it is deeper, and let down your nets to catch some fish." "Master," Simon replied, "we worked hard all last night and didn't catch a thing. But if you say so, I'll let the nets down again." And this time their nets were so full of fish they began to tear! A shout for help brought their partners in the other boat, and soon both boats were filled with fish and on the verge of sinking. (Luke 5:4–7)**

Remember what Jesus said in **Luke 6:38** about the return on giving "running over?" That is exactly what happened to Peter. He caught more fish than he could handle. Even when they brought all the boats together there were so many fish the boats were overloaded. Now that is a great example of God's abundance!

GOD DIDN'T TELL ME TO GIVE!

Should you wait to hear the Holy Spirit impress you with specific instructions before you give? Of course not. This is an area of life where God has made His will clear. God put His will about giving into His word, the Bible. You can make a decision to give on your own regardless of whether you hear a specific word from the Holy Spirit.

> **You must each decide in your heart how much to give...(2 Cor. 9:7)**

We can make our own decisions about giving. We can each decide, or purpose, in our own hearts about whether or not to give to a need. My neighbor came over one summer day and asked if I had any wasp spray. I knew I had a can in my tool room. It would have been ridiculous for me to say, "I need to pray about this to see if God will speak to me about letting you use my wasp spray." He had a need and I could supply the need. I made a decision to give him the can of wasp spray. I purposed in my heart to help him.

I believe there are times when God will impress on your heart to give to a certain need. When He does that, you should obey His prompting and give as directed. However, that is not the only time you can give. You can cooperate with God by deciding in your heart to give to meet a need.

I Don't Want To

Your attitude when you give is also important to God. He can look inside you and see your true feelings about giving. If you want to cooperate with God for a financial return on your giving, you have to be happy about what you are doing. If you are angry and really don't want to help, God can see that. He is looking for people who have **decided** they want to give and are **happy** about it.

> **You must each decide in your heart how much to give. And don't give reluctantly or in response to pressure. "For God loves a person who gives cheerfully." (2 Corinthians 9:7)**

Sometimes we feel pressured to give. Maybe a minister badgers you about giving in a service until you finally give in. You take a $20 bill from your wallet or purse and throw it into the offering container as if to say, "There you go, God. I hope you're happy!" Well, He is **not** happy. He is not happy because **you** are not happy. He wants you to **want** to give. You are not cooperating with God if you have a stinking attitude about your giving. Look at this verse again in the Amplified translation.

> **Let each one [give] as he has made up his own mind and purposed in his heart, not reluctantly or sorrowfully or under compulsion, for**

> **God loves (He takes pleasure in, prizes above other things, and is unwilling to abandon or to do without) a cheerful (joyous, "prompt to do it") giver [whose heart is in his giving]. (2 Corinthians 9:7)(AMP)**

I believe the Bible definition of prosperity is this:

"Having enough to meet your own needs and enough left over to help someone else."

God wants to use **you** to bring financial blessing to others in need. When money flows from God **through** you to help others, you are cooperating with God and He is exalted.

> **Yes, you will be enriched in every way so that you can always be generous. And when we take your gifts to those who need them, they will thank God. (2 Corinthians 9:11)**

IS THAT EVERYTHING?

This chapter has covered the basic principles about cooperating with God concerning your giving and your attitude concerning giving. There is much more we could cover about prosperity, but this book has a specific focus on cooperating with God in different areas. Financial prosperity also is affected by your education and training; your wise stewardship of the money God sends your way; your understanding of God's direction for your vocation in life; your willingness to be diligent in your work habits and not be lazy. Those topics are all important. However, the end result of all your efforts will always be affected by whether or not you cooperate with God by releasing a portion of your money to be a blessing to someone else.

6. Soulwinning

I was 25 years old and had been a Christian since I was eight. Not one time had I lead a person into a salvation experience. I knew I was supposed to be a soulwinner. Why did I hesitate? Why did it seem so difficult? Because I didn't know what to say. I had no confidence I could convince someone to become a Christian. Maybe you have felt the same way.

Part of my problem was I thought I had to do it all myself. I did not realize that soulwinning was a cooperative effort with God. I thought I had to have great sales ability and know every Scripture in the Bible. After all, wasn't that kind of thing for full-time evangelists? I realized I needed to change. My wife and I made a commitment to learn how to be soulwinners. Soulwinners are wise people. Don't you want to be a wise person?

> **The fruit of the righteous is a tree of life, and he who wins souls is wise. (Proverbs 11:30) (NKJV)**

Nobody can be saved until they make a decision to trust Jesus for their salvation. No matter what religious group a person identifies with, each individual is responsible for making a decision for Jesus. Some people think living a reasonably good life will get them into Heaven. Some people think believing in God in some form is all that is required. Some people believe that belonging to a Christian denomination causes them to be saved. Many people have been fooled into thinking they are Christians even though they have never made a decision to trust Jesus for their salvation. Somebody has to tell them the truth. **You** are that somebody.

I remember sitting next to a lady on an airplane. In our brief, introductory conversation, I found out she was a pharmacist living in Washington, D.C. I asked her if she was interested in spiritual things and she replied, "I am a Presbyterian." I asked her what she would say if someone asked her, "What is a Christian?" She hesitated and said something about going to church or believing in God, and finally said, "I'm not sure what you are getting at." I asked her what she would say if she died and stood at the gates to Heaven and Jesus asked her why He should let her in. Once again, she hesitated and said something like, "I would say that I believe in God and went to church and tried to live a good life." I said to her, "Ma'am, I'm sorry, but that won't get you into Heaven." I asked her if I could share a few Scriptures with her to help her understand how to be saved and she said, "Yes."

I shared the simple gospel message with her. I used *Romans 3:23* to establish that every person has sinned. I used *Romans 6:23* to help her see that sin produces separation from God, eternal life is only available through Jesus and salvation is a gift that can only be received or rejected. I used *Ephesians 2:8–9* to reinforce that salvation is a gift and that no one can boast of having earned eternal life. I went to ***John 1:12*** to help her see when the gift of eternal life through Jesus is received, she would become a child of God. I ended with ***Revelation 3:20*** where Jesus said He knocks at the door wanting to come in. When I asked her if she would open the door of her heart to receive Jesus as her Savior, she said, "Yes." I led her in a salvation prayer and this precious young woman was born again.

This woman thought that she was a Christian. She thought that, because she identified with a particular denomination, she was secure. There are many people just like her. If you ask them a question about their religious beliefs they may say, "I am an Episcopalian," or, "I am a Methodist, Baptist, Pentecostal, Catholic" or any number of religious groups. No one has told them the truth. All I did was tell her the truth. You can do the same thing.

There is power in the message of the gospel. The gospel is the good news of what Jesus did for us. The gospel has the power to change people from the inside out. Many people try to change their behavior to please God and earn their salvation. Most of the religions of the world provide instructions in changing your behavior to please God. They will teach if you do everything just right, God may decide He likes you and will do something good for you someday. Changing yourself from the outside in is the message of most religions.

The gospel message is that God Himself will change a person on the inside. Once the inside is changed, the way a person lives will change. We are not talking about "turning over a new leaf" and trying to live better. Remember that the gospel message you are sharing has **power** to change a person.

> **For I am not ashamed of this Good News about Christ. It is the power of God at work, saving everyone who believes—the Jew first and also the Gentile. (Romans 1:16)**

THE HOLY SPIRIT

God is on your side when you are sharing the gospel with a person. He wants the person to be saved more than you do. He has not left you on your own. Remember that God lives inside you in the person of the Holy Spirit if you are born again. Jesus said the Holy Spirit will always be there to help you. This is especially true when you are telling someone about Jesus. The Holy Spirit will help you do the things you cannot do on your own.

> **And I will ask the Father, and he will give you another Advocate, who will never leave you. He is the Holy Spirit, who leads into all truth. The world cannot receive him, because it isn't looking for him and doesn't recognize him. But you know him, because he lives with you now and later will be in you. (John 14:16-17)**

Before a person can be saved, he must admit he has sinned. When you begin to talk to a person about Jesus, you can expect the Holy Spirit to convict that person of sin.

> **And when he comes, he will convict the world of its sin, and of God's righteousness, and of the coming judgment. (John 16:8).**

You don't have to point out all of a person's sins. The Holy Spirit will make a person know in his heart that he has sinned. Once a person admits he has sinned, the Holy Spirit can begin to draw him to God. You can tell him about God, but the Holy Spirit has to work in his heart to encourage him to turn his life over to Jesus.

After 30 minutes of jogging, my body develops a desire for water. No one has to convince me that water would be a good thing for me. I have a natural desire. As you begin to talk about Jesus, the Holy Spirit works with you to increase a person's desire for God.

> **For no one can come to me unless the Father who sent me draws them to me... (John 6:44)**

THE WORD OF GOD

Cooperating with God when you witness also involves using the Word of God, the Bible. Some people consider the Bible to be a boring history book. The Bible is much more than that. Remember that the Bible is "inspired" by God. That means the Holy Spirit working "in" the writers brought forth God's revelation. That is why the Bible is called the "Word of God." It also means God's life is in His Word.

> **For the word of God is alive and powerful. It is sharper than the sharpest two-edged sword, cutting between soul and spirit, between joint and marrow. It exposes our innermost thoughts and desires. (Hebrews 4:12)**

The Word of God is "powerful!" It is totally unlike anybody else's word. It works like a sword to reveal the truth about a person's life. A sword is a sharp instrument that is used to cut.

I remember dissecting a frog in biology class. The sharp instrument I used to open up the frog was a scalpel. The scalpel enabled me to see what was inside the frog. The Word of God works in a similar way. When you share the Word of God with a person, that Word penetrates deep into the heart and mind. The Word of God reveals the truth about what is in his heart. The Word of God is empowered with God's life. You don't have to depend on your persuasive words alone. Just use God's words which are full of His life and power.

Even if you don't see immediate results, know that you have planted a seed of truth into a person's spirit. That seed will remain inside a person. Natural seeds will rot and decay over time. They will eventually lose their usefulness and not be able to produce fruit. The seed of the Word of God is incorruptible. It is not capable of dying.

> **having been born again, not of corruptible seed but incorruptible, through the word of God which lives and abides forever, (1 Peter 1:23)(NKJV)**

The Holy Spirit will bring that living word out of their spirit to remind them of the truth long after you have gone. It is impossible for them to get rid of the eternal Word of God which you have planted inside them. Days, weeks, even years later, the Holy Spirit can remind them of what you said. Even if someone else is present when God reaps the harvest of that person's soul, you can play a vital part by planting the eternal seed of the Word of God.

> **I planted the seed in your hearts, and Apollos watered it, but it was God who made it grow. It's not important who does the planting, or who does the watering. What's important is that God makes the seed grow. The one who plants and the one who waters work together with the same purpose. And both will be rewarded for their own hard work. (1 Corinthians 3:6–8)**

A Plan

Most people don't share the gospel because they don't know what to say. I was the same way. The solution to that problem is to have a plan. A plan is a series of questions and answers which will bring a person to a point of decision. There are several advantages to having a plan.

1. <u>A plan gives you confidence</u>. I am very confident when I drive around the city where I live. I don't hesitate. I am not tentative. I know where I am going and I know how to get there. I can tell when I am behind a visitor. They drive slowly. They keep looking at street signs to see where they are. They are not confident because they are not familiar with this city. A plan gives you the ability to speak with confidence and authority.

2. <u>You can control the conversation</u>. Instead of rambling on and on, waiting for the right opportunity to talk about Jesus, you are in control. You take the conversation in the direction you want it to go.

3. <u>You know what you are going to say next</u>. Instead of stumbling around searching for words, you know exactly what you will say.

4. <u>You don't need to know what the Bible says about every subject</u>. You control the conversation and keep it from wandering down a side road about some religious question that has no bearing on your topic. Because you know in advance what you are going to talk about, you will arrive at your destination quickly.

There is no such thing as one perfect plan that will work for everybody. Many wonderful books are available which will help you develop a plan that works for you and your personality. Look for one that enables you to easily move a conversation into the subject of Jesus, regardless of how it started. Or you could use the plan I described in my conversation on the plane. I am not talking about going door-to-door witnessing. I am referring to a way to deliberately turn a conversation into a witnessing opportunity. You could ask your pastor for help, go to your Christian bookstore and find a plan that works for you or even search on the internet for help.

GOD IS GOOD

Most of the time, people need to hear about how good God is, not how bad He will punish them for their sins. Sinners know they are sinners. They need to know that God still loves them even though He doesn't like the way they are living. When folks find out God wants to forgive them instead of punish them, they are more likely to turn toward God. The word "repent" means to turn and go another direction.

> **Don't you see how wonderfully kind, tolerant, and patient God is with you? Does this mean nothing to you? Can't you see that his kindness is intended to turn you from your sin? (Romans 2:4)**

The goodness and kindness of God is revealed in what Jesus said about Himself. Jesus made it clear that His primary purpose was not to point out people's sins, but to provide a way of escape from the penalty of those sins.

> **God sent his Son into the world not to judge the world, but to save the world through him. (John 3:17)**

Ask For A Decision

Nobody gets saved by accident. Every person must make a decision to trust Jesus and be born again. Many people don't understand a decision is required. The ultimate goal of witnessing is to help a person realize they have to decide "yes" or "no" to trust Jesus for salvation. Jesus is the focal point of the gospel. You can cooperate with God by asking for a decision to trust **Jesus**, not to join your church or denomination.

> **For there is only one God and one Mediator who can reconcile God and humanity—the man Christ Jesus. (1 Timothy 2:5)**

Jesus, the man, the Savior, is to be lifted up as the remedy for sin. Not His teachings. Not church membership. Not baptism. Not a dress code. Not living a perfect life. Eternal life is a gift and it is only available through Jesus. A gift cannot be earned or it is no longer a gift. A gift can only be received or rejected. When you offer the gift of eternal life, you must ask for a decision. "Will you receive this gift or will you reject it?"

> **For the wages of sin is death, but the free gift of God is eternal life through Christ Jesus our Lord. (Romans 6:23)**

When you offer that wonderful gift of eternal life, Jesus will work with you to draw that person to Himself. You are not alone. Jesus, the Holy Spirit and the Word of God are all working with you to persuade this person to be born into the kingdom of God.

DO IT NOW

You can see people born into the kingdom of God if you will decide to cooperate with God and do it now. It is easy to find an excuse why you can't share the gospel with someone. "I don't want to offend them." "They may not be ready." "This isn't the right place." "This isn't a good time." Jesus told us the harvest of souls is ready right now. Not later, but now. God is waiting on us to reap the harvest.

> **Then Jesus explained: "My nourishment comes from doing the will of God, who sent me, and from finishing his work. You know the saying, 'Four months between planting and harvest.' But I say, wake up and look around. The fields are already ripe for harvest. (John 4:34–35)**

Many years ago, when I was still working as a consulting engineer, I had lunch with another engineer who was from Kuwait. He was in our office temporarily working on a project. We went to a cafeteria and, as we ate our food, I began to share with him about Jesus. His facial expression never changed as I shared the truth of the gospel. He didn't look excited. He didn't look interested. He just looked at me while I talked. I asked him if he would like to pray to receive Jesus as his Savior. He nodded his head, yes.

As we sat at our table in the middle of a crowded cafeteria during the lunch hour, he repeated a salvation prayer and was saved. He never even bowed his head. He just kept looking intently at me as I led him in a prayer. It didn't look like this would be a good time. We were in a public place with a lot of people who could see us. He came from a non-Christian country. I could have offended him by telling him about Jesus. But I knew that God didn't want him to spend one more day separated from God. I knew that the best time for him to be saved was "now."

> **For God says, "At just the right time, I heard you. On the day of salvation, I helped you." Indeed, the "right time" is now. Today is the day of salvation. (2 Corinthians 6:2)**

I believe God is going to send you to someone who needs to be saved "right now!" Don't let the opportunity pass you by.

7. Marriage

MARRIAGE IS SUPPOSED TO BE A DREAM COMing true. We commit our life to the person we feel God has given us. Surely our problems will be minimal. We will easily resolve all differences with love and mercy and forgiveness. Each day will be like heaven on earth. Our spouse will fulfill all our desires. Our relationship will be a shining example to the world of a perfect marriage. At least that is the way we think it will be. Sometimes it doesn't work out quite like a fairy tale.

Less than two years after the wedding, our marriage was in critical condition. We had dated for three and a half years in college and were engaged for three months before we were married. You would think all the problems would be worked out by then. Karen's expectations and my behavior were miles apart. Our problems at home even caused Karen to be tempted to start a relationship with another man.

We were both Christians. I was saved when I was eight and Karen when she was fifteen. We went to Sunday school and church together every week. But it looked like the marriage would soon be over. We went to our pastor for counseling. He did the best he knew how. He talked about "I'm OK, You're OK" which was a popular book at the time. The counseling did no good at all.

Karen had met some children at a laundromat who told her how great their church was. We decided to visit that church. This pastor, Billy Joe Daugherty, was much nearer our age than our pastor. He preached a lot differently, too. He wasn't louder or more demonstrative, but he preached a message of power and hope. Since we weren't getting help from our own church, we scheduled an appointment with Pastor Daugherty.

Pastor Daugherty didn't talk about psychology. He opened his Bible and began to show us what

God said in His Word. He told us our feelings were subject to change. He said if we would believe the Word of God that God would enable us to put our marriage back together. He told us we had a part to play. We had to trust God **first** and then our feelings would begin to change. That counseling session was in 1979. And we are still married!

How did it happen? How could a marriage in such severe trouble survive? How could feelings which had grown cold turn back into deep love and affection? The answer lies in understanding how to cooperate with God. The first step is to find out the will of God concerning marriage and then choose to agree with His will.

The Marriage Covenant

The first relationship God created was between Himself and mankind. He created the first man, Adam, breathed into him an eternal spirit and began to talk to him. This relationship is the most important and was intended to last for eternity. Marriage was the second relationship God created. God saw that Adam was lonely and needed a partner to share his life with. So God put Adam to sleep and created Eve.

This relationship between a man and a woman is a covenant relationship. A covenant is the strongest agreement known to man. Covenant relationships have been around for thousands of years. When two tribes, countries or individuals cut a covenant together they are saying, "Whatever I have, if you need it, it is yours." "And whatever you have, if I need it, it is mine."

The marriage covenant should be taken seriously. Ending a marriage is not the same as a boyfriend/girlfriend breaking up in high school. The covenant of marriage should be honored and not taken lightly. You may have to fight for your marriage. Some days it may seem like it will never work and it would be easier to walk out, hire a lawyer and end it. This is one way to cooperate with God concerning your marriage. Ask God to help you keep His love in your heart for your spouse.

Joined Together

In the case of the marriage covenant, the two parties become joined together as one unit instead of two people.

> **This explains why a man leaves his father and mother and is joined to his wife, and the two are united into one. (Genesis 2:24)**

One way to cooperate with God's plan for marriage is to begin a new life as a couple. When a man and woman marry, they should both leave their respective family units. The scripture quoted above clearly states that truth by using the man as an example. It is extremely difficult to bond together as husband and wife if you continue to live with, or spend too much time with, either set of parents. Parents can't help being parents. They want to help their children along. They want to give advice and it is hard for a son or daughter not to listen.

But for a marriage to work, God said to **leave** your father and mother and join yourself to your spouse. That doesn't mean you stop listening to your parents. It just means you don't live with them anymore. You have to learn to work out your own problems without running to mama or daddy every time the going gets rough. Your parents are usually going to be on your side in a dispute with your spouse. But what if you are the one who needs to change? You are more likely to learn to depend on God and each other if you leave your family and start fresh with your spouse.

A covenant relationship was designed to only be broken by the death of one of the parties. God's intention was that the marriage covenant relationship would only be terminated by the death of one of the partners. His plan was that no human being would be the cause of separating a married couple. Jesus explained this when some religious leaders asked Him about the acceptability of divorce. He referred back to God's words recorded in Genesis.

> "Haven't you read the Scriptures?" Jesus replied. "They record that from the beginning 'God made them male and female.' And he said, 'This explains why a man leaves his father and mother and is joined to his wife, and the two are united into one.' Since they are no longer two but one, let no one split apart what God has joined together." (Matthew 19:4-6)

God's ideal plan for the length of a marriage relationship was also reflected in the Old Testament law He gave the nation of Israel through Moses.

> For example, when a woman marries, the law binds her to her husband as long as he is alive. But if he dies, the laws of marriage no longer apply to her. (Romans 7:2)

What If I Am Already Divorced?

Some of you are asking that question right now. This is a chapter on cooperating with God to see your marriage work. This is not a book on the theology and dynamics of marriage, divorce and remarriage. There are many reasons why marriages end in divorce. Some are legitimate and some are not. If you are divorced, I obviously don't know why your marriage didn't last. My purpose in writing this chapter is not to make you feel bad about a failed marriage. My reason for writing is to help you learn to cooperate with God so your current marriage or next marriage will not fail. I can't change your past. I can only help you with your future. If you were part of the cause for a failed marriage, than ask Jesus to forgive you for your mistakes. He doesn't want to sentence you to a life of remorse and misery. He wants to set you free from errors of the past.

> **But if we confess our sins to him, he is faithful and just to forgive us our sins and to cleanse us from all wickedness. (1 John 1:9)**

By all means, learn from the mistakes of your past so you won't repeat them. But don't let your failures dominate your life. You have to forgive yourself, your former spouse and anyone else involved in the mistakes of your past. Once you have chosen to forgive everyone involved, let the past stay in the past and determine to achieve better results with your future.

> I don't mean to say that I have already achieved these things or that I have already reached perfection. But I press on to possess that perfection for which Christ Jesus first possessed me. No, dear brothers and sisters, I have not achieved it, but <u>I focus on this one thing: Forgetting the past and looking forward to what lies ahead</u>, I press on to reach the end of the race and receive the heavenly prize for which God, through Christ Jesus, is calling us. (Philippians 3:12-14)

What Do You Think?

Part of cooperating with God for your marriage to last is to be careful what you think about. When a marriage goes through a rocky period, it can be easy to think about running away from the problems by getting a divorce. You may begin to imagine what it would be like to be free from your spouse. Your mind may present an argument for a much better life without the restrictions of marriage. Or your eye may begin to wander and you think that another person you know would make a much better spouse. But those thoughts are contrary to God's thoughts. God's plan is for your marriage to work.

> **casting down arguments and every high thing that exalts itself against the knowledge of God, bringing every thought into captivity to the obedience of Christ, (2 Corinthians 10:5) (NKJV)**

I get sales calls at home just like you do. Usually I am polite when I decline their offer. However, sometimes, if I am in a hurry or in the middle of something important, I am not so polite. In those times I don't let the caller get into the sales pitch. I am not willing to listen so I just say, "I'm not interested, thank you" and hang up the phone.

You have to be that way with thoughts about divorce or infidelity. Don't allow Satan to paint a perverted picture in your mind. Just say, "I'm not interested!" and cast that thought down just like you would hang up the phone. God has given **you** the authority to do that. **You** can control what goes on in your mind. You must cooperate with God to keep your thoughts in line with God's thoughts. Think about the good things in your marriage. Think about why you got married. Think about the goodness of God. Replace those negative thoughts with God's thoughts.

> **And now, dear brothers and sisters, one final thing. Fix your thoughts on what is true, and honorable, and right, and pure, and lovely, and admirable. Think about things that are excellent and worthy of praise. (Philippians 4:8)**

You also have to be careful about who you listen to. If you hang around folks who have left their spouses for only selfish reasons, you can have your thinking corrupted. They may want you to do the same thing they did. Talking you into doing the same thing may help them justify what they have done. Make sure you are only influenced by God's ideas and not by other people.

> **Don't be fooled by those who say such things, for "bad company corrupts good character." (1 Corinthians 15:33)**

THE FEELING IS GONE

When Karen and I were dating, we really enjoyed being together. We looked forward to going out to eat or to a movie or a sporting event. We really **felt good** when we were together. But after two years of marriage, the feelings we both once had for each other began to wane. Karen was tempted to see another man. I found other things to occupy my time. If we had made a decision based on our feelings, we would be divorced now. We learned something very important during this time, however. We learned that **feelings are subject to change**. God can help your feelings to change. He can change your desires.

> **Take delight in the Lord, and he will give you your heart's desires. (Psalm 37:4)**

If your desire for your spouse is not what it used to be, God has an answer. **Delight yourself in the Lord**. Put your attention on God. Make sure He is the most important relationship in your life. Increase your prayer time. Increase your time reading the Bible—that is the primary way God will speak to you. Make sure you are regularly attending a good church. Get your focus off yourself and your problems.

Your part is to *"Take delight in the Lord..."* God's part is to put His desires in your heart. His desire is that your marriage would be strengthened and not end. His desire is that your love for your spouse would increase. Once you do your part, He will do His part. Once you begin to cooperate with God, He will begin to put His desires in your heart and give you the power to follow those desires.

For God is working in you, giving you the desire and the power to do what pleases him. (Philippians 2:13)

When Karen and I realized this truth, we began to focus on God. He began to change our will, our desires, our "want to." Some of you may say, "I just don't want to try to make my marriage work." God can change your "want to" if you will just give Him a chance. We did what we had to do. We humbled ourselves before God and asked for help with our feelings. God did His part and, over time, restored the feelings we once had for each other. He can do the same thing for you.

8. Healing

MANY PEOPLE BELIEVE THAT GOD <u>CAN</u> STILL heal, but have never seen anybody healed. Many people believe God still heals <u>today</u>, but are hesitant to pray for a sick person to be healed. Many sick people believe God heals <u>some</u> people, but that He doesn't want to heal <u>them</u>. Is it totally up to God to determine who is healed and who isn't? Or is it possible that we could have something to do with it? Could it be that we have to cooperate with God to put ourselves in position to see His healing power manifested?

Most of the confusion about healing has to do with discerning God's will. Some people take positions at opposite ends of the spectrum. One view says, "God doesn't heal miraculously anymore because He has provided doctors and medical science." Another view says, "If you do not get healed miraculously, it is because you do not have enough faith." Maybe the answers about healing are not as simple as either of those extreme positions.

God's Covenants

God has manifested His healing power throughout recorded history. Under the Old Covenant, which He established to govern His relationship with the nation of Israel, God provided healing.

> **"You must serve only the Lord your God. If you do, I will bless you with food and water, and I will protect you from illness. There will be no miscarriages or infertility in your land, and I will give you long, full lives. (Exodus 23:25-26)**

Jesus came to establish a New Covenant with mankind. This new covenant would be better than the Old Covenant. The most important thing the

New Covenant added was the blessing of forgiveness and removal of sins by trusting in Jesus. However, the New Covenant which Jesus established did not do away with the Old Covenant blessings. It made them better by adding to them.

> **But now Jesus, our High Priest, has been given a ministry that is far superior to the old priesthood, for he is the one who mediates for us a far better covenant with God, based on better promises (Hebrews 8:6)**

God's Compassion

The Bible says nothing about eliminating the Old Covenant promises of healing when Jesus established the New Covenant. Through Jesus' public ministry, He demonstrated God's healing power. The healing miracles Jesus performed were certainly signs attesting to Him being the Son of God. However, Jesus also healed people for another reason. Healing demonstrated the compassion of God.

Compassion motivates a person to do something beyond just feeling sorry about someone's condition.

> Jesus saw the huge crowd as he stepped from the boat, and <u>he had compassion</u> on them and healed their sick. (Matthew 14:14)

> Now as they went out of Jericho, a great multitude followed Him. And behold, two blind men sitting by the road, when they heard that Jesus was passing by, cried out, saying, "Have mercy on us, O Lord, Son of David!" Then the multitude warned them that they should be quiet; but they cried out all the more, saying, "Have mercy on us, O Lord, Son of David!" So Jesus stood still and called them, and said, "What do you want Me to do for you?" They said to Him, "Lord, that our eyes may be opened." <u>So Jesus had compassion</u> and touched their eyes. And immediately their eyes received sight, and they followed Him. (Matthew 20:29–34) (NKJV)

Healing Methods

The Bible describes several different ways to receive healing from God. The mistake some people make is in limiting God to only one way to manifest His healing. We can sometimes confuse His **methods** with His **will**. Just because He doesn't heal in the **way** I would have preferred doesn't mean He doesn't **want** to heal or that He **won't** heal. There may be other ways to cooperate with God to see His healing manifested. Here are a few.

1. The Gifts of Healings

This is the most well-known method for healing. This method of healing is totally dependent on God's will. The only thing we can do to cooperate with God to receive healing this way is to be around someone whom God uses in this gift.

> **But the manifestation of the Spirit is given to each one for the profit of all: for to one**

> **is given the word of wisdom through the Spirit, to another the word of knowledge through the same Spirit, to another faith by the same Spirit, <u>to another gifts of healings by the same Spirit</u>, to another the working of miracles, to another prophecy, to another discerning of spirits, to another different kinds of tongues, to another the interpretation of tongues. But one and the same Spirit works all these things, <u>distributing to each one individually as He wills</u>. (1 Corinthians 12:7–11)(NKJV)**

This gift has operated throughout history as God has supernaturally equipped healing evangelists to preach and demonstrate God's healing power in countries all over the world. In larger crusades, thousands of people attend open-air crusades to hear the gospel message about Jesus and many of them are healed of physical ailments. They are healed because God chooses to manifest His healing power through men and women through the gifts of healings. The healings alleviate physical needs and demonstrate the goodness and power of God. People's hearts are opened and receptive when the opportunity is given to receive Jesus as their Savior and Lord. This gift will continue to operate as long as the church is on the earth.

> **And God has appointed these in the church: first apostles, second prophets, third teachers, after that miracles, then <u>gifts of healings</u>, helps, administrations, varieties of tongues. (1 Corinthians 12:28) (NKJV)**

The healing gifts flow through a person to the one needing healing. The person needing healing is the recipient of the gift. This gift operates as the Spirit of God wills. That is why a person God regularly uses in this gift can't just go into a hospital, turn on the gift and heal everybody. It only operates when God wants it to operate. Jesus operated in this gift and even He couldn't make it work whenever He wanted to heal everybody. Here is an example.

> Afterward Jesus returned to Jerusalem for one of the Jewish holy days. Inside the city, near the Sheep Gate, was the pool of Bethesda, with five covered porches. Crowds of sick people—blind, lame, or paralyzed—lay on the porches. One of the men lying there had been sick for thirty-eight years. When Jesus saw him and knew he had been ill for a long time, he asked him, "Would you like to get well?" "I can't, sir," the sick man said, "for I have no one to put me into the pool when the water bubbles up. Someone else always gets there ahead of me." Jesus told him, "Stand up, pick up your mat, and walk!" Instantly, the man was healed! He rolled up his sleeping mat and began walking! But this miracle happened on the Sabbath, (John 5:1–9)

Notice there were <u>crowds</u> of sick people there. But Jesus only healed one person in those crowds. Why? Because the gift of healing was in operation and God made the decision to heal only one person through this gift on that day. Jesus didn't turn it on and heal the great multitude. He could only do what the Holy Spirit wanted to do. If this was the only way to receive healing, there would be very little we could do to cooperate with God. But this isn't the only way.

2. Prayer of Elders

I helped move a piano one time. A piano is very heavy. There is no way I can move one by myself. I am not strong enough. I need help to lift a load that heavy. When several people gather around the piano, the load is lighter for each person. We can accomplish much more by combining our strength.

Sometimes when you are sick you need help. You may be too tired to resist the sickness. The physical symptoms may have drained your natural energy. You may be spiritually tired from other battles you have been fighting. You may need to combine the spiritual strength of several people to help lift the sickness off your body.

> **Are any of you sick? You should call for the elders of the church to come and pray over you, anointing you with oil in the name of the Lord. Such a prayer offered in faith will heal the sick, and the Lord will make you well. And if you have committed any sins, you will be forgiven. Confess your sins to each other and pray for each other so that you may be healed. The earnest prayer of a righteous person has great power and produces wonderful results. (James 5:14-16)**

You can cooperate with God to receive healing by calling on the elders of your local church to pray with you. Who are the elders? Are they the oldest people in your church? In this instance, I believe the elders are spiritually mature people. Elders have been through their own battles and have been strengthened because of it. They can join their faith with yours to gain the victory over the physical sickness which is troubling you. Oil is a symbol of the Holy Spirit. Anointing with oil is symbolic of the presence of God. When the oil is rubbed on your body, it is a tangible reminder that God's healing power is flowing during this time of prayer.

3. Laying Hands On The Sick

Jesus gave us some instructions before He left the earth to ascend to the Father in Heaven.

> These miraculous signs will accompany those who believe: They will cast out demons in my name, and they will speak in new languages. They will be able to handle snakes with safety, and if they drink anything poisonous, it won't hurt them. They will be able to place their hands on the sick, and they will be healed."
> (Mark 16:17-18)

Jesus said certain signs would follow "those who believe." Jesus did not want His ministry to end because He was leaving the earth physically to go to Heaven. He told "believers" they were to continue

His ministry activities even though He would not be physically with them. He said to do these things by using His name. In today's world, we understand what He did as granting the "power of attorney."

If I owned a number of corporations and had to be out of the country for several months, I could grant my assistant the "power of attorney." I would spell out in detail what he was authorized to do in my absence. His responsibility would be to act the same way I would act if I were still in the country. He could use my name so my business affairs could continue.

That is what Jesus has done for believers. He has granted us the authority to use His name to do the same thing He would do if He were still here physically. What did Jesus do when He encountered a person controlled by a demon? He cast out the demon. That is why He said believers can do the same thing. Jesus referred to demon spirits as "serpents" in *Luke 10:17–20*. We can "take up serpents," or demons, and cast them out. We can speak to demon spirits and cast them out just like Jesus did.

What did Jesus do when He was around sick people? He healed them. That is why Jesus said believers *"will lay hands on the sick and they will recover."* He wants His healing ministry to continue through the church, the believers, the Body of Christ. In order for believers to see people healed they have to cooperate with God according to His word. What does His word say we have to do?

A. BE A BELIEVER

Notice that Jesus said *"And these signs will follow those who believe..."* He said the signs would follow **believers**. This means you have to believe in Jesus as your savior and as a healer. One reason many Christians never see anyone healed is because they do not believe Jesus is still healing. Believers have to believe or they are not believers! If you don't believe in healing, don't bother praying for sick people. The signs, such as healing, only follow those who believe.

B. BELIEVE IN HIS NAME

Part of our cooperation with God is not just to believe in Jesus as savior and healer but to believe in the power and authority of the "name of Jesus." The name of Jesus represents the person of Jesus. He has delegated to believers the authority to use His name to accomplish His will. One area of His will is to bring healing to those who are sick.

> **And these signs will follow those who believe: <u>In My name</u>...they will lay hands on the sick, and they will recover." (Mark 16:17-18) (NKJV)**

There are other Scriptures that emphasize the importance of believing in the power of Jesus' name. One of them we have already looked at from a different angle.

> **...You should call for the elders of the church to come and pray over you, anointing you with oil <u>in the name of the Lord</u>. (James 5:14)**

What is the name of the Lord? The name of the Lord is "Jesus." The elders are to pray for healing in the name of Jesus. But also notice what kind of a prayer must be prayed.

> **"Such a prayer offered in faith will heal the sick, and the Lord will make you well...." (James 5:15)**

A prayer offered in faith is a believing prayer. There must be a believing prayer in the name of Jesus before the sick person will be made well. The elders have a part to play in bringing healing to the sick person. They are required to believe in the authority and power of the name of Jesus when they pray.

C. PRAY FOR THE SICK

Here is how cooperating with God works for bringing healing to another. Jesus said that believers *"will lay hands on the sick, and they will recover."* That means you must be willing to lay hands on a sick person. As an act of your will, you must lay hands on the sick and pray and believe in the name of Jesus. If you want to see sick people healed, you have to lay hands on sick people. When you pray a believing prayer, God's healing power can be freed to flow into the sick person's body. Your part is to lay hands on the sick. God's part is to bring the recovery. If you don't do your part, God won't do His part.

The most common reason for not laying hands on the sick is the fear that the person will not be healed. We are afraid we will be embarrassed if it doesn't work. I understand that feeling, but consider this illustration. Let's assume you had a new disease no one had heard about before. You spent all your money going to doctors and they all told you there is no cure and you have only three months to live.

But you hear about a doctor who has been working on a cure for this dreaded disease. You quickly make your way to this doctor's office for an exam. He checks you out thoroughly and says, "I have studied this disease for several years." "I have a medication which may cure your disease and allow you to live out your life." "However, I don't believe I will give it to you because I am not sure it will work and I would not want you to be upset with me."

What would you say to that doctor? I know what I would say. "Give me that medication!" "This may be my only hope!"

So the doctor gives you the medication and it doesn't work. You don't get better. The doctor says, "I don't understand why it didn't work." "I wanted it to work." The doctor is terribly disappointed. But at least he can go to sleep at night knowing he did everything he knew to do to help you.

We should have the same attitude about praying for the sick. We can't concern ourselves with thoughts about "What if it doesn't work?" The command we received from Jesus is to lay hands on the sick and believe in the power and authority of His name. We can only do our part. The recovery part is God's responsibility.

If you lay hands on a sick person and believe with everything within you for them to be healed, you have done your part. If they don't get healed, at least you can go to bed at night knowing you did everything you knew to do to help. We will never have all the answers about why some people are not healed. We can only do our part.

4. Praying In Agreement

God has given great power to those who will unify their faith. Even in decisions that are in opposition to the will of God, there is great power in unity. Following the great flood, Noah's descendants were multiplying. God's plan was that they would separate into colonies to replenish the earth. Everyone spoke the same language and had the same dialect. However, the people decided to stay in one place to build a city instead of separating. They also decided to build a monument to themselves to celebrate their own greatness.

> At one time all the people of the world spoke the same language and used the same words. As the people migrated to the east, they found a plain in the land of Babylonia and settled there. They began saying to each other, "Let's make bricks and harden them with fire." (In this region bricks were used instead of stone, and tar was used for mortar.) Then

they said, "Come, let's build a great city for ourselves with a tower that reaches into the sky. This will make us famous and keep us from being scattered all over the world." (Genesis 11:1-4)

God was not pleased with their actions. He knew, however, that there was great power in unity. He knew they could accomplish great things if they were all in agreement. So God took matters into His own hands to force them to disperse as He intended. He forced the people to divide by giving them each their own language which others could not understand.

But the Lord came down to look at the city and the tower the people were building. "Look!" he said. "The people are united, and they all speak the same language. After this, nothing they set out to do will be impossible for them! Come, let's go down and confuse the people with different languages. Then they won't be able to understand each other."

> In that way, the Lord scattered them all over the world, and they stopped building the city. That is why the city was called Babel, because that is where the Lord confused the people with different languages. In this way he scattered them all over the world. (Genesis 11:5–9)

That same power of unity can be used for good. When two or more believers come together to pray a prayer of agreement, great power is made available. This is one way to cooperate with God for healing. Jesus made this statement:

> "I also tell you this: If two of you agree here on earth concerning anything you ask, my Father in heaven will do it for you. For where two or three gather together as my followers, I am there among them." (Matthew 18:19–20)

The critical part of this instruction is the word "agree." Both people must be praying and believing the same thing. That is why when someone asks me to pray for them I ask them, "What about?" I want to be sure I am in agreement with what they are praying. If you are visiting a person in the hospital to encourage them and pray for them, you should find out what you can agree on. If you decide to pray for a miraculous, instant healing, and they want to pray for a successful surgery, you are not in agreement. Find out what you can agree on because agreement in prayer brings God's power on the scene.

Notice in verse 20 Jesus said, *"For where two or three gather together as my followers, I am there among them."* Verse 20 follows verse 19 so He hasn't changed the subject. He is still talking about agreement in prayer. Jesus said if we will agree in prayer then He will be in the middle of those two or three people, causing their prayer of agreement to come to pass. We misuse this verse sometimes to encourage people when we have a low turnout for a church service. We like to say, "Well, Jesus said if there are only two or three, He is there." He wasn't talking about low attendance at a church meeting. The Bible says in 1 Corinthians 6:19, *"Don't you realize that*

your body is the temple of the Holy Spirit, who lives in you and was given to you by God? ..." You don't have to get two or three Christians together for God to show up. He lives inside every believer. If only one person shows up, God is there. Jesus was talking about being in the middle of a prayer of agreement to cause that prayer to be answered.

5. Proper Nutrition

God has provided for our every need. He has included food for us to eat. Fruits and vegetables were created by God to nourish our bodies. The proper food enables our bodies to function at peak capacity. Unfortunately, in America, we have too many choices concerning what we can eat. We have food we call "junk food." Junk food is easy to buy, quick to eat and pleasing to the taste. But most of it is not natural or good for the body. What good does it do to pray for healing if poor eating habits are the root cause for our sickness? If a person is healed and continues to feed on unhealthy, unnatural food, many times the sickness will come back.

I know this isn't easy to do. I have struggled with this issue. I could buy a dozen peanut butter cookies from the grocery store bakery and eat all of them within an hour. It isn't fun to discipline your body, but it is necessary. You can cooperate with God to stay healthy by being disciplined in what you eat. That doesn't mean you never eat anything that is fun and unhealthy. It just means you eat those things in moderation along with plenty of healthy foods.

> Don't you realize that in a race everyone runs, but only one person gets the prize? So run to win! All athletes are disciplined in their training. They do it to win a prize that will fade away, but we do it for an eternal prize. So I run with purpose in every step. I am not just shadowboxing. <u>I discipline my body like an athlete, training it to do what it should</u>. Otherwise, I fear that after preaching to others I myself might be disqualified. (1 Corinthians 9:24–27)

6. Doctors

Any truth can be stretched beyond its intended use and become distorted. Jesus is still supernaturally healing folks today. That is a wonderful truth. However, that truth is distorted if we take the position that it is a <u>sin</u> to consult a medical doctor. Some distort this issue the other direction by saying God <u>only</u> heals through doctors. So which one is right?

The truth is that God wants you well. You are limited in how you can serve Him if you are suffering from sickness or disease. Doctors want you well, too. So it seems that God and doctors both want the same thing. If God did not want you well, you would be sinning by going to a doctor and trying to get well. You are not a failure if you go see a doctor. The important thing is to go to God **first** and ask Him for healing. Make sure you have done everything possible to put yourself in position to receive God's healing power. If you still aren't getting better, or you are in an emergency situation, then go see a doctor. But trust God to work through the doctor to help you regain your health.

9. Preparing To Serve

When I was in my 20s, I used to umpire high school baseball games in Oklahoma. Umpiring baseball was a hard job both mentally and physically. Half the people thought I was wrong on every close play so I had to listen to those folks yelling at me. Also, summers in Oklahoma are blazing hot. The thermometer normally tops one-hundred degrees for several weeks. The equipment I had to wear made it even worse.

I wore a bulky chest protector inside my shirt. I strapped a pair of shin guards underneath my long pants. I laced a pair of steel-toed shoes over a pair of thick socks. After adding a hat and mask, I was ready to step out into the bright sunshine and sweat my guts out. The umpire's dressing room was air conditioned. It was tough to leave that comfortable environment. I looked forward to going back there and feeling the refreshing chill on my sweat-soaked body between games.

In addition to the clothes and equipment, I hung a bag for spare baseballs on my belt and held a counter in my hand to keep track of balls, strikes and outs. The last thing I needed was a thorough knowledge of the rules of the game. I kept that in my head.

You have to be equipped to umpire baseball. Sometimes people in the stands think they can do a better job. They never get the chance because they aren't willing to pay the price to be equipped. The clothes and protective gear cost money. The knowledge of the rules comes from intense study. Understanding how to be at the right place on the field to see the play comes from experience. Good umpires don't just show up. Good umpires do what it takes to develop into the best umpire they can be.

Christians who impact other people's lives don't just show up either. God doesn't choose some people and tell the rest they can float through life with no responsibility to help anyone else. Christians who do something to count for eternity have learned to cooperate with God to prepare. They pay the price to mature and acquire the skills necessary to help change people's lives.

Jesus intends for every believer to do the work of the ministry. He has a place for you to serve which will bring you great joy. He wants you to enjoy serving Him passionately.

> **So, my dear brothers and sisters, be strong and immovable. Always work enthusiastically for the Lord, for you know that nothing you do for the Lord is ever useless. (1 Corinthians 15:58)**

Believers have to be equipped to be effective just like an umpire has to be equipped. God-given ability is a starting place, but productive Christians go beyond depending on God to do everything. Saying to God that you are available is the first step. But nothing much happens until you begin to take action to prepare for God to work through you in a special way.

Training

People who are successful in the business world realize the importance of training. Training includes both teaching and action. You can gain knowledge both from your experience and from the experiences of others.

My dad built a doghouse for one of our bird dogs one summer. "Here is a can of paint," he said. "Paint the doghouse while I'm gone to work and we'll put it in the dog pen when I get home."

I was only ten years old and had never done any painting. I brushed a coat of white paint on the bare wood and waited for it to dry. It looked horrible. It was splotchy and uneven. I thought I had ruined the doghouse. I was in agony the rest of the day as I watched the clock. I dreaded my dad coming home from work to find out I was a failure. My heart pounded as he drove into the driveway. I cried as I took him into the back yard to show him the ugly doghouse.

"You didn't do anything wrong," said my dad. "Bare wood always looks that way after only one coat of paint."

He had neglected to tell me I would have to put on two coats of paint to make it look nice. That was very important information to leave out! I finished the job the next day and the doghouse looked great. I had been taught and I had actually done the work. I was now equipped to do the work of painting a doghouse.

Christians are gifted in different ways. Some people can sing well. Some people can organize and administrate. Others can teach. The list goes on. A God-given ability, however, can lie dormant and never be of benefit to anyone if it is not developed.

I remember the first time I stood in front of a group of people to preach. I was nervous. I was jumpy. I had a hard time speaking for 15 minutes. The next time I spoke, I did a little better. Now, decades later, I enjoy speaking in public because I have done it enough to gain confidence. Experience is part of being equipped. You have to force yourself to exercise your gift in order to improve.

How do you get started now that you realize you should be equipped to do the work of the ministry? Here are seven ideas that will help you cooperate with God to fulfill His will in doing the work of ministry.

1. Define Your Gifts

> **In his grace, God has given us different gifts for doing certain things well... (Romans 12:6)**

You can't develop a gift until you know what it is. Begin to write down areas of ministry that interest you. Are you more excited about a singer or a Bible teacher coming to your church? Would you rather take food to someone who is sick or pray with a person at the altar? Are you more comfortable talking one-on-one, in front of a group or working alone in the background?

Listing your preferences to questions like these will enable you to more clearly define your strengths and the areas you will be most effective. Writing down what you **don't** like is as helpful as writing down what you **do** like. Then you can avoid working in areas in which you have no passion or gifting. Your Christian bookstore is a source for more detailed information about determining your spiritual gifts.

2. Talk To Your Pastor

> Now these are the gifts Christ gave to the church: the apostles, the prophets, the evangelists, and the pastors and teachers. Their responsibility is to equip God's people to do his work and build up the church, the body of Christ. (Ephesians 4:11-12)

God has provided ministry gifts to equip believers. Ministry gifts are people (such as pastors and teachers) that Jesus has gifted to teach, train and motivate others. Tell your pastor about your decision to develop yourself to work in the ministry. Your pastor is responsible to God for your spiritual growth and will have a great interest in helping you. He/she may have noticed some of your strong points that you overlooked. Be sure to listen to what your pastor says. He/she will assist you in both identifying and **developing** your gifts. That means you may not start off in a position of leadership. You might not be ready. You may need to begin by assisting another ministry leader.

3. Volunteer To Work—Then Do It!

> **Work willingly at whatever you do, as though you were working for the Lord rather than for people. (Colossians 3:23)**

> **Never be lazy, but work hard and serve the Lord enthusiastically. (Romans 12:11)**

I remember a lady talking to me after her first visit to our church one Sunday.

"I love this church and I really want to get involved here," she said.

I told her I wanted to discuss her desire when we had more time. I wanted to get to know her a little better to see where she would best fit in. I never saw that lady in church again! There is a big difference between talking and doing! One of the biggest challenges a pastor faces is finding faithful people. Volunteer ministry activity should be taken seriously.

If you make a commitment, then keep that commitment as if it were the highest paying job you ever had. I had a Sunday school teacher not show up for her class for three weeks in a row and never tell anyone she wasn't coming. You wouldn't do that with a job. Don't do it in the ministry. It would be better not to start at all if you are going to quit when the going gets tough. Remember that you are working for God, not people.

4. Study To Develop Your Gifts

> **Work hard so you can present yourself to God and receive his approval. Be a good worker, one who does not need to be ashamed**

**and who correctly explains the word of truth.
(2 Timothy 2:15)**

Take the initiative to increase your understanding of your gift. If you are involved with outreach activity, read books or listen to teaching on soul winning. If you are helping in the youth ministry, read or listen to instruction about ministering to teens. Read about groups and individuals who are actively ministering in the area of your interest. Find seminar video or audio recordings you can purchase or borrow. Treat it as if you were starting a new career.

These tools will provide a base of understanding from which to build. Then, the work you do in the ministry will provide opportunities to apply what you have learned from your study.

5. Attend Seminars and Conferences

**Let us think of ways to motivate one another to acts of love and good works.
(Hebrews 10:24)**

Conferences and seminars about your chosen area of ministry provide more than just information. You will be motivated by the interaction. You will meet others who are facing the same challenges. As you mature, you can also be an encourager to other frustrated beginners.

You may find something close-by which would help you. However, attending some conferences could be expensive and time-consuming. Allow your pastor or ministry leader to help you determine the right ones for you. I once attended a writer's conference 400 miles from my home. It took four days out of my schedule and several hundred dollars. But it was worth every minute and every dollar. The wisdom that can be gained from people who are doing what you want to do is invaluable.

6. Develop Friendships

Plans go wrong for lack of advice; many advisers bring success. (Proverbs 15:22)

As a writer, it is always helpful to let someone else look over my work. Because I am so close to the product, it is easy to overlook problem areas. That is why writers need editors.

When you are deeply involved in a particular area of ministry, it may be difficult for you to discern your weak spots. Having friends from other churches or ministries who will be candid with you can be a great help. Tell them everything you are doing and be willing to listen to their comments without defending yourself. They may not always be right, but if they are truly friends you should carefully weigh their suggestions and insights.

7. BE WILLING TO CHANGE

> ... Yes, I try to find common ground with everyone, doing everything I can to save some. I do everything to spread the Good News and share in its blessings. (1 Corinthians 9:22–23)

There is one statement that will absolutely keep you from fulfilling God's plan for your life and ministry. If you catch yourself thinking or saying this, you have just put the brakes on your journey with God:

"But I've never done it that way before!"

God's eternal purpose of salvation never changes. However, His methods do change. Much of what we do in ministry is based on what has been done in the past. However, society changes. Technology changes. We have to be willing to change, if necessary, to stay up-to-date and reach people in today's culture. There is a difference between change and compromise. We don't compromise and accept immoral behavior because the world is more tolerant of sin. But we need to understand the difference between the truth of the gospel, which will never change, and the methods we use to present the gospel.

I know of a parent who claimed that rap music was from the devil. This person said it was impossible to have Christian rap music and that it was like having a "Christian liquor store" - there is no such thing. This is an example of refusing to work through today's culture. The style of music may not be to your liking, but if the words proclaim the gospel, it is a way to reach a certain segment of young people.

Think of something as simple as singing in church. Decades ago, the standard method was to provide hymnals for church members to use to read the words and music. Then churches updated to use a device called an overhead projector to put the words on a screen or a wall. Now we are able to use computers in conjunction with projectors to project words and video onto massive screens. Who knows what the future will hold? We are still worshiping God in our singing. Only the methods have changed.

Decide To Prepare

I had to make a decision to be equipped to become an umpire. I had to commit the time to study the rule book. I had to spend time around experienced umpires to learn how to handle situations that occur in a game. I had to invest my money into clothes and equipment to look like an umpire and be protected from injury.

In order to cooperate with God, **You** have to make a decision to become equipped to do the work of the ministry. **You** have to invest your time and money to learn how to develop your gifts. The results of your efforts will have an eternal impact on the lives God will lead you to touch.

10. Holy Spirit Power

John the Baptist was a cousin to Jesus. John was continually preaching that people should repent and turn away from sin. God sent John the Baptist to prepare the way for Jesus. John was a wild dude, but he knew he was not the main attraction. He knew that once Jesus came on the scene all the attention would be on Jesus.

> His clothes were woven from coarse camel hair, and he wore a leather belt around his waist. For food he ate locusts and wild honey. John announced: "Someone is coming soon who is greater than I am—so much greater that I'm not even worthy to stoop down like a slave and untie the straps of his sandals. I baptize

> you with water, but he will baptize you with the Holy Spirit!" (Mark 1:6–8)

John the Baptist talked about how Jesus would baptize people with the Holy Spirit. What is the baptism with the Holy Spirit? Who can receive this baptism? Does Jesus select only certain people to have this experience? Do we have anything to do with it or does Jesus just do it when He wants to?

Many people believe the baptism of the Holy Spirit occurs when a person is born again. If that is correct, we only need to trust Jesus for our salvation to have this experience. The born again experience certainly involves the work of the Holy Spirit.

> Jesus replied, "I assure you, no one can enter the Kingdom of God without being born of water and the Spirit. Humans can reproduce only human life, but the Holy Spirit gives birth to spiritual life. So don't be surprised when I say, 'You must be born again.' The wind blows wherever it wants. Just as you can hear the wind but

> can't tell where it comes from or where it is going, so you can't explain how people are born of the Spirit." (John 3:5-8)

The Holy Spirit causes the human spirit to be reborn. The spirit which is darkened and stained with sin is made new, pure and holy. The mistakes of the past are totally removed and the new Christian is given a fresh start.

> Therefore, if anyone is in Christ, he is a new creation; old things have passed away; behold, all things have become new. (2 Corinthians 5:17)(NKJV)

The new birth causes a person to become a part of the body of Christ. The Holy Spirit places the believer into the body of Christ.

> Some of us are Jews, some are Gentiles, some are slaves, and some are free. But we have all been baptized into one body by one

> Spirit, and we all share the same Spirit. (1 Corinthians 12:13)

The Holy Spirit also comes to live inside the new believer.

> But you are not controlled by your sinful nature. You are controlled by the Spirit if you have the Spirit of God living in you. (And remember that those who do not have the Spirit of Christ living in them do not belong to him at all.) (Romans 8:9)

Our conversion experience causes us to be baptized <u>into</u> the body of Christ <u>by</u> the Holy Spirit. Remember, however, that John the Baptist said <u>Jesus</u> would baptize <u>with</u> the Holy Spirit. The word "baptize" means, "to immerse, dip or submerge." When you are saved, you are immersed into and become a part of the body of Christ. To be baptized in the Holy Spirit would require us to be immersed or submerged in the Holy Spirit. Those are two separate experiences. If I take a drink of water, I have water inside me. However, if I jump into a swimming pool I don't just have water in me. I am immersed in water. Jesus wants all believers to be immersed in the power of the Holy Spirit.

The first experience, being saved, is required before we can have the second experience of being baptized in the Holy Spirit. The Bible uses wine as a symbol of the Holy Spirit. Your conversion creates a new container for the wine of the Holy Spirit. New wine required a new container. In Bible days, people stored wine in animal skins. Used skins became stiff and brittle. New skins were supple and could take the expansion that comes when new wine is stored. Jesus talked about this.

> **"And no one puts new wine into old wineskins. For the wine would burst the wineskins, and the wine and the skins would both be lost. New wine calls for new wineskins." (Mark 2:22)**

Peter preached a sermon on the day of Pentecost and explained it was necessary to be saved before you can receive the Holy Spirit.

> **Peter replied, "Each of you must repent of your sins and turn to God, and be baptized in the name of Jesus Christ for the forgiveness of your sins. Then you will receive the gift of the Holy Spirit. (Acts 2:38)**

What happens when a person receives the baptism of the Holy Spirit? On the day Jesus ascended back to heaven He gave His followers some instructions.

> **Once when he was eating with them, he commanded them, "Do not leave Jerusalem until the Father sends you the gift he promised, as I told you before. John baptized with water, but in just a few days you will be baptized with the Holy Spirit." (Acts 1:4–5)**

The Holy Spirit Arrives

Jesus told them the day was coming when they would experience what John the Baptist talked about. For this group, the baptism of the Holy Spirit was going to occur in just a few days. Ten days later, 120 of Jesus' followers were in Jerusalem waiting for the promise of the Holy Spirit to be fulfilled.

On the day of Pentecost all the believers were meeting together in one place. Suddenly, there was a sound from heaven like the roaring of a mighty windstorm, and it filled the house where they were sitting. Then, what looked like flames or tongues of fire appeared and settled on each of them. And everyone present was filled with the Holy Spirit and began speaking in other languages, as the Holy Spirit gave them this ability. At that time there were devout Jews from every nation living in Jerusalem. When they heard the loud noise, everyone came running, and they were bewildered

> **to hear their own languages being spoken by the believers. (Acts 2:1-6)**

These believers began to speak in languages, or tongues, they had not learned. This was a physical evidence of a spiritual experience. They had been immersed in the power of the Holy Spirit. The outward manifestation was speaking in unknown languages, or tongues. This same manifestation is shown in several instances of believers receiving the baptism of the Holy Spirit.

Peter was sent by the Holy Spirit to preach the gospel to a man named Cornelius. Cornelius was an unsaved man but he loved God, generously gave money to the poor and prayed regularly. God saw his heart of love for God and people and told him in a vision to send for Peter. Peter went to the house of Cornelius and found Cornelius had gathered a crowd of relatives and friends. As Peter preached about Jesus, those in the house believed on Jesus, were saved and received the baptism of the Holy Spirit. How did everyone know they had received the baptism of the Holy Spirit? Because the same physical manifestation of speaking in unknown languages, or tongues, occurred that had taken place on the day of Pentecost.

> Even as Peter was saying these things, the Holy Spirit fell upon all who were listening to the message. The Jewish believers who came with Peter were amazed that the gift of the Holy Spirit had been poured out on the Gentiles, too. For they heard them speaking in other tongues and praising God. Then Peter asked, "Can anyone object to their being baptized, now that they have received the Holy Spirit just as we did?" So he gave orders for them to be baptized in the name of Jesus Christ. Afterward Cornelius asked him to stay with them for several days. (Acts 10:44–48)

Twenty years after the initial outpouring of the Holy Spirit that occurred on the day of Pentecost, Paul encountered a group of disciples in Ephesus.

There are two interesting things to look at in the account of this incident.

> While Apollos was in Corinth, Paul traveled through the interior regions until he reached Ephesus, on the coast, where he found several believers. "Did you receive the Holy Spirit when you believed?" he asked them. "No," they replied, "we haven't even heard that there is a Holy Spirit." "Then what baptism did you experience?" he asked. And they replied, "The baptism of John." Paul said, "John's baptism called for repentance from sin. But John himself told the people to believe in the one who would come later, meaning Jesus." As soon as they heard this, they were baptized in the name of the Lord Jesus. Then when Paul laid his hands on them, the Holy Spirit came on them, and they spoke in other tongues and prophesied. There were about twelve men in all. (Acts 19:1–7)

These folks apparently had been baptized in water by John the Baptist as a sign of repentance from sin. Paul explained the gospel to them; made sure they believed on Jesus as Savior and had them baptized in water to signify their identification with Jesus and His death, burial and resurrection. Then Paul laid hands on them so they could receive the baptism of the Holy Spirit. What happened after they received the baptism of the Holy Spirit? They spoke with tongues. The same manifestation was repeated.

Notice also that when Paul first approached them he asked, *"Did you receive the Holy Spirit when you believed?"* Some people's viewpoint is that we receive everything there is to receive from the Holy Spirit when we are saved. But Paul asked if they had received, *"since you believed."* Obviously there is something more to receive from God after believing on Jesus for your salvation. Otherwise Paul would not have asked such a question and he would not have laid his hands on them <u>after</u> they were saved to receive the baptism of the Holy Spirit.

Another example is found after Philip preached a great crusade at Samaria. Many people were saved and wonderful miracles had occurred. But apparently the people had not been instructed in receiving the baptism of the Holy Spirit. Because of that, Peter and John were sent to these folks, who were already saved and baptized in water, to lay hands on them so they could receive the wonderful experience of the baptism of the Holy Spirit.

> **When the apostles in Jerusalem heard that the people of Samaria had accepted God's message, they sent Peter and John there. As soon as they arrived, they prayed for these new believers to receive the Holy Spirit. The Holy Spirit had not yet come upon any of them, for they had only been baptized in the name of the Lord Jesus. Then Peter and John laid their hands upon these believers, and they received the Holy Spirit. (Acts 8:14–17)**

Why Is It Important?

What is the purpose of the baptism of the Holy Spirit? Is it just to be able to speak in an unknown language, in tongues? Not at all. Praying in tongues is a benefit of the experience, not the primary reason for it. The primary reason, according to Jesus, is to receive the power of the Holy Spirit for service. A good example is when Peter stood up and preached a great sermon after being empowered with the Holy Spirit. Over 3,000 people were saved as a result of that sermon!

> But you will receive power when the Holy Spirit comes upon you. And you will be my witnesses, telling people about me everywhere—in Jerusalem, throughout Judea, in Samaria, and to the ends of the earth." (Acts 1:8)

> Those who believed what Peter said were baptized and added to the church that day—about 3,000 in all. (Acts 2:41)

We need the help of the Holy Spirit to carry on Jesus' ministry as part of His body. He delegated His authority to us to use His name to act as He would act if He were still here physically. We need the same power source Jesus had, which is the Holy Spirit. Jesus did no miracles or healings until He was empowered by the Holy Spirit when He was baptized in water by John the Baptist.

> **One day Jesus came from Nazareth in Galilee, and John baptized him in the Jordan River. As Jesus came up out of the water, he saw the heavens splitting apart and the Holy Spirit descending on him like a dove. And a voice from heaven said, "You are my dearly loved Son, and you bring me great joy." (Mark 1:9-11)**

I provided all that teaching to establish the following truths from the word of God about the baptism of the Holy Spirit. Now we can talk about how we must cooperate with God to receive Holy Spirit power.

1. It is for every believer.
2. It is a separate experience that occurs after being born again.
3. The primary reason is to provide power to serve God more effectively.
4. The physical evidence of this experience, for those who will fully cooperate with God, is the ability to pray in tongues.

Is It All Up to Jesus?

Now we need to look at another aspect of this experience. The initial outpouring occurred on the day of Pentecost. This was the beginning of the fulfillment of a prophecy by the prophet Joel. After being empowered by the Holy Spirit on the day of Pentecost, Peter begins to preach a powerful sermon which explains what has just happened.

Then Peter stepped forward with the eleven other apostles and shouted to the crowd, "Listen carefully, all of you, fellow

> Jews and residents of Jerusalem! Make no mistake about this. These people are not drunk, as some of you are assuming. Nine o'clock in the morning is much too early for that. No, what you see was predicted long ago by the prophet Joel: 'In the last days,' God says, 'I will pour out my Spirit upon all people. Your sons and daughters will prophesy. Your young men will see visions, and your old men will dream dreams. In those days I will pour out my Spirit even on my servants—men and women alike—and they will prophesy. (Acts 2:14-18)

This is all part of God's master plan for mankind. If it is part of God's plan, I want to get in on it. I hope you do too. How does a person receive the baptism of the Holy Spirit? You receive by asking. Some have been afraid to ask God for the fullness of the Holy Spirit. Some have even thought that you might get a demon spirit if you ask for it. But what does Jesus say?

10. Holy Spirit Power — 181

> "And so I tell you, keep on asking, and you will receive what you ask for. Keep on seeking, and you will find. Keep on knocking, and the door will be opened to you. For everyone who asks, receives. Everyone who seeks, finds. And to everyone who knocks, the door will be opened.
> "You fathers—if your children ask for a fish, do you give them a snake instead? Or if they ask for an egg, do you give them a scorpion? Of course not! So if you sinful people know how to give good gifts to your children, <u>how much more will your heavenly Father give the Holy Spirit to those who ask him.</u>" (Luke 11:9–13)

God will not substitute a counterfeit for the Holy Spirit when you ask for Him. You will receive exactly what you ask for. Remember, you are asking to be baptized or immersed in the **Holy Spirit**. Some people get confused and ask God for the gift of tongues. The ability to pray in tongues will come when you are empowered by the Holy Spirit. The Holy Spirit should be the object of your attention, not praying in tongues. Now notice what happened to people as described in the Scriptures we looked at earlier.

> **And <u>they</u> were all filled with the Holy Spirit and <u>began to speak</u> with other tongues as the Spirit gave them the <u>utterance</u>. (Acts 2:4) (NKJV)**

I underlined certain words in this Scripture for emphasis. Who did the speaking and who gave the utterance? Each person did his or her own speaking. The Holy Spirit did not do the speaking. The individuals did the speaking. What did the Holy Spirit do? The Holy Spirit gave them the utterance, the words to speak.

This is where most folks get confused about receiving the baptism of the Holy Spirit. I have prayed with many people who stand rigidly in front of me waiting for the Holy Spirit to take them over and **make** them pray in tongues. It doesn't happen that way. The Holy Spirit isn't going to **make** you pray in tongues. He **helps** you to pray.

You have to cooperate with Him and submit to Him. His part is to give you the utterance, the words to speak. He will put the words in your spirit. These will be words you have never spoken before. They will be a new language. These will be words that sound funny to your mind. These words will **stay** in your spirit unless you are willing to open your mouth and speak them out.

Some would say, "But I don't want it to be me speaking." Well, who else is it going to be? On the day of Pentecost, "they" began to speak the words the Holy Spirit put inside of them. You have a part to play and God has a part to play. His part is to give you the words. Your part is to speak those words. If you don't speak them, it's not God's fault, is it?

I have prayed with many people who want to say "thank you, Jesus" or "hallelujah" or something similar over and over. You cannot speak in two languages at the same time. You have to stop talking in your native language if you want to start praying in tongues.

For they heard them speaking in other tongues and praising God...(Acts 10:46)

> Then when Paul laid his hands on them, the Holy Spirit came on them, and they spoke in other tongues and prophesied. (Acts 19:6)

The Apostle Paul wrote:

> I thank God that I speak in tongues more than any of you. (1 Corinthians 14:18)

What About Prayer?

Cooperating with God to speak in tongues doesn't end with the initial experience of the baptism of the Holy Spirit. God has provided the Holy Spirit to help us all of our lives. The Holy Spirit will never abandon a Christian.

> And I will ask the Father, and he will give you another Advocate, who will never leave you. He is the Holy Spirit, who leads into all truth...(John 14:16-17)

There is more than one operation of the gift of tongues. Paul wrote a letter to the church at Corinth in which he explained in great detail the various operations and manifestations of the Holy Spirit. This is how he described it:

> **There are diversities of gifts, but the same Spirit. There are differences of ministries, but the same Lord. And there are diversities of activities, but it is the same God who works all in all. But the manifestation of the Spirit is given to each one for the profit of all: (1 Corinthians 12:4-6)(NKJV)**

The primary operational use of the gift of tongues is for the believer's private prayer life.

> **For if you have the ability to speak in tongues, you will be talking only to God, since people won't be able to understand you. You will be speaking by the power of the Spirit, but it will all be mysterious. (1 Corinthians 14:2)**

When I pray in tongues I am speaking mysteries because my mind does not understand what I am saying. The Holy Spirit is **helping me** to pray for things my mind does not comprehend. Have you ever faced a struggle in life where you did not know what to pray? I have. How do you pray for relatives or friends who live far away and you don't know what they need? We need **help** in times like these. Jesus said the Holy Spirit would be our **Helper**.

When we submit to the Holy Spirit and allow Him to help us pray, He will always be there. Since the Holy Spirit is God, and since He gives us the words to pray, we know we will always be praying the perfect will of God when we pray in tongues.

Who Chooses When We Pray?

When can we pray in tongues? Do we have to wait for a special anointing to fall on us? Is it only when we are emotionally charged up? Does it have to be in a church service where everyone is singing and dancing and making a lot of noise? Or is it possible that we can pray in tongues whenever we choose?

> **So anyone who speaks in tongues should pray also for the ability to interpret what has been said. For if I pray in tongues, my spirit is praying, but I don't understand what I am saying. Well then, what shall I do? I will pray in the spirit, and I will also pray in words I understand. I will sing in the spirit, and I will also sing in words I understand. (1 Corinthians 14:13-15)**

Paul made it clear that praying in tongues is an operation of the Holy Spirit working inside our human spirit. He said his spirit was doing the praying and not his mind. The spirit and the mind are two separate entities.

The Holy Spirit helps us pray by putting words of prayer in our spirit. We cooperate with Him by speaking those words out even though our mind doesn't understand the language we are speaking. The mind will not be involved unless the Holy Spirit gives us the interpretation of what we are praying. That is why Paul said to ask God for the interpretation when we pray in tongues. God does not have to give us the interpretation every time we pray. We have to trust that God knows what is best for us and is helping us pray for His perfect will to be accomplished.

In the Scripture above, Paul asks the question (paraphrased), "Since I don't know what I am saying when I pray in tongues what should I do?" Then he answers the question by saying we should pray in two different ways. We should pray for those things we know to pray for with our native language. But we should also pray for those things we don't know how to pray about by praying in tongues. Notice that Paul did not place any qualifications on when he could pray in either his native language or in tongues. He said it was an act of his will either way. Look at it again with underlining I have added for clarification.

So anyone who speaks in tongues should pray also for the ability to interpret what has been said. For if <u>I pray</u> in tongues, my spirit is praying, but I don't understand what I am saying. Well then, what shall I do? <u>I will</u> pray in the spirit, and <u>I will</u> also pray in words I understand.

> **I will sing in the spirit, and I will also sing in words I understand. (1 Corinthians 14:13–15)**

Paul said **he** decided, as an act of his will, when he would pray, whether in his native language or in the spirit, in tongues. Many have been taught that the gift of tongues can only operate as the Holy Spirit wills. There is an **operation** of the gift of tongues that **does** only operate as the Spirit wills. That is an operation where God speaks a message **to a group of believers** through an individual speaking in tongues, and then gives the interpretation of that message so everyone at the meeting can understand.

> **Well, my brothers and sisters, let's summarize. When you meet together, one will sing, another will teach, another will tell some special revelation God has given, one will speak in tongues, and another will interpret what is said. But everything that is done must strengthen all of you. No more than two or three should speak in tongues. They**

> **must speak one at a time, and someone must interpret what they say. But if no one is present who can interpret, they must be silent in your church meeting and speak in tongues to God privately. (1 Corinthians 14:26–28)**

We cannot make the Holy Spirit **speak a message** to a church group whenever we want to. That is an operation we cannot control. However, every believer can **pray** in the Holy Spirit at any time. Notice this Scripture says if there is no interpreter a person can still speak to God. As we read in *1 Corinthians 14:2*, when we pray in tongues we are speaking directly to God.

The Holy Spirit is always available to help us pray. I cannot imagine a time when I would ask the Holy Spirit to help me pray and He would say "No, I refuse to help you pray." Praying in the spirit is a cooperative effort between God, the Holy Spirit, and a believer. It is a gift which will continue to be necessary until Jesus, the perfect one, returns and we are able to speak with Him face to face.

> Love never fails. But whether there are prophecies, they will fail; whether there are tongues, they will cease; whether there is knowledge, it will vanish away. For we know in part and we prophesy in part. But when that which is perfect has come, then that which is in part will be done away. When I was a child, I spoke as a child, I understood as a child, I thought as a child; but when I became a man, I put away childish things. For now we see in a mirror, dimly, but then face to face. Now I know in part, but then I shall know just as I also am known. (1 Corinthians 13:8-12)(NKJV)

The baptism of the Holy Spirit is not something to be feared. It is a blessing, a help to every believer who desires it. If you will cooperate with Jesus, He will empower you with the Holy Spirit to enable you to live a more effective life of service and provide you a powerful means of communicating with the Father.

ABOUT THE AUTHOR

RANDY CLARK has been teaching the truths of the Bible since graduating from Victory Bible Institute in Tulsa, Oklahoma in 1980.

He has served as a Pastor, Bible School Instructor, Church Planter and Christian Television Station Manager. His ministry has also included a weekly television program and a daily radio outreach.

Randy's ministry travels have taken him across the United States and into foreign countries as close as Canada and Mexico and as far away as Indonesia and Ukraine.

He is the author of numerous books and magazine articles and is the founder of Randy Clark Ministries, a worldwide teaching and training ministry. For more resources from the author visit his website at:

www.RandyClark.info

If this book was a help to you, please go to the Amazon.com listing for the book and leave a review. This will encourage others to take advantage of the information and inspiration found within these pages. This book is also available in Kindle and Audible formats through Amazon.com.

www.ingramcontent.com/pod-product-compliance
Lightning Source LLC
Chambersburg PA
CBHW030321080526
44584CB00012B/656